CROWOOD METALWORKING GUIDES

WORKHOLDING FOR MACHINISTS

CROWOOD METALWORKING GUIDES

WORKHOLDING FOR MACHINISTS

TIM STEVENS

THE CROWOOD PRESS

First published in 2017 by
The Crowood Press Ltd
Ramsbury, Marlborough
Wiltshire SN8 2HR

www.crowood.com

British Library Cataloguing-in-Publication Data
A catalogue record for this book is available from the British Library.

ISBN 978 1 78500 238 0

Man is a tool-using animal … without tools he is nothing, with tools he is all.
Thomas Carlyle (1795–1881)

Safety is of the utmost importance in every aspect of metalworking. The practical workshop procedures and the tools and equipment used in metalworking are potentially dangerous. Tools should be used in strict accordance with the manufacturer's recommended procedures and current health and safety regulations. The author and publisher cannot accept responsibility for any accident or injury caused by following the advice given in this book.

Typeset by Derek Doyle & Associates, Shaw Heath
Printed and bound in Malaysia by Times Offset (M) Sdn Bhd

Contents

1 Introduction

This book is intended primarily to help those who are relatively new to the work of the machinist; the intention is to bring together in one volume a wide range of work-holding methods along with the principles behind them, many of which go back to the days before electric power was invented, even in some cases to the chair bodger in the woods and the clockmaker in the remotest valleys of the Alps. It is also intended to help the raw beginner in this line of work and to form a guide for those whose skills, and perhaps workshops, are not yet fully developed. Do not be surprised, then, to find an explanation of some things you know to be perfectly obvious. Too often, what is obvious to one is something another has never even thought about. The writers of manuals themselves are not always free from this sort of thinking. How many times do we read advice in a manual to use a suitable tool or carry out a task in the normal way? It is hoped that in these pages you will find out (or be reminded) what a suitable tool might be, and what the normal way is, and more than that, you may begin more clearly to understand why and to fill one or two of the gaps in your knowledge.

To start this process, we need to be clear about what we mean. Engineering has its jargon, like all trades and professions, so where there is a word that might not be familiar or one used in a special engineering or scientific sense, it will be shown first in quotes 'thus'. The term 'normal', which we have just used in an everyday sense, for example, also has a particular (and quite distinct) meaning in engineering drawing: a 'normal' line is one at right angles to a surface or to another line. The term normalized is also used in describing a particular heat treatment of steel. Most such terms are explained in detail in the glossary towards the end of the book. It may help, too, if we are clear about other details of word use. This book is written in British English, so you can expect the spellings of words like centre and vice to be English.

The term 'work holding' generally means the method of fixing the job on which you are about to carry out machining, so that it is held firmly and accurately in relation to the machine. Accurately includes holding the work in exactly the right place, at the right height and at the right angle, as well as in a way that prevents movement away from this position during further work. In this book the coverage will be extended slightly to include holding the tool properly, as there are operations, such as milling, where the tool moves quickly under power while the job moves slowly, or not at all. Both need to be secure. In addition, there are manual operations, such as filing and polishing, which properly speaking, are distinct from machining but the processes, the problems and solutions are closely related just the same.

There are several reasons to carry out work holding in an organized and considered way. These are the problems you need to avoid:

- Damage to you and others nearby.
- Damage to the machine.
- Damage to the cutting tool itself.
- Damage to the workpiece.
- Failure to achieve the required precision or surface finish.

These are not, in fact, separate problems: any one is very likely to come with others too.

Other things we need to get right depend on the nature of the job. Does it need to be part finished on one machine, taken to another for more work and returned to be finished off? In this case it may be helpful to hold the part using areas that are not affected by subsequent work or, alternatively, arrange to hold the work for the second and third operations relying on areas machined in the first. An alternative approach might involve a separate part made up specially to hold the work so that it can be located accurately on different machines. Perhaps there are several workpieces needing the same operation on each in turn. Do these workpieces need to be exactly the same, so that any of them can replace another without extra work? Again it might help to make a special 'jig' to hold the work rather than relying solely on off-the-shelf holding tools.

These are all aspects of repeatability and this need can impose further complications unless it is thought about well in advance. Some jobs present real problems with work holding because of their delicacy, or shape, or the need to machine to a fine finish all over. Others need to have milled faces, drilled holes and turned diameters in very exact relationships, even though these operations are normally carried out on separate machines.

The time to find or work out the solutions is before you start. When cutting a length from a stock bar, for example, might it be useful to cut it a few centimetres too long, so that the spare end can be used to hold the work until the very last operation? Could you make a pair of parts from one piece of stock, each machined by holding the other end, and then separated? Is it possible to arrange the sequence of operations so that, for example, a set of holes is drilled first, so that they can be used to bolt the part to a fixed surface and locate it accurately for the next operations? Perhaps the holes could be made undersize and tapped to enable the job to be bolted down from the other side, with a final drilling or boring out to the drawing size? Would it help to produce accurately positioned and reamed holes as locations for further

operations even though the drawing only calls for a position within a sixteenth of an inch? Should the holes be done last, with the work, and the hole positions located accurately in relation to the newly machined surfaces? Might it be worthwhile to make, first, a fixture to which the work could be attached and moved as an assembly from lathe to mill to drill and back? Have you got all the fittings and clamps in the sizes you are going to need?

Getting this right at an early stage will avoid having to start work on a separate job part way through the first, so that the time taken in setting up accurately is not needed twice. An hour or two of careful thought at the start really can save a lot of time and frustration later. If you make a list of the operations with the details of work holding, mentally working through each operation in turn, it can help to ensure that the order is the most sensible and this will act as a reminder when you return to the shed, even if it is a few days later.

If your workpiece is irregular, or has a rough or knobbly surface, holding it to get started is going to need particular care. However accurate your vice or chuck and however much force you apply to the handle, unless you follow the rules, the work will not be held firmly. Not that these rules are set out anywhere in a machinists' ten commandments, you understand, they are learnt like anything else, by reading, by talking with others and by making mistakes. For example, a vice – any vice – is designed to hold objects with flat, parallel surfaces. In the same way, a chuck is intended to hold work that is cylindrical, or perhaps a prism with three, or

Fig. 1.1 A clamping kit like this in a size to match the slots in your machine is a good start for many work-holding jobs. AXMINSTER TOOL CENTRE LTD

four, sides. This is fairly obvious, when you think about it. The nearer you can get to the conditions the makers had in mind, the more secure will be your workpiece. To hold a workpiece onto a flat surface, whether a faceplate or a milling table, there needs to be a flat surface on the work or at least something that acts in the same way. If only one, or two, of the surface knobbles on your expensive casting actually rests on the flat surface, movement during machining is going to be inevitable. Three lumps in contact, making a triangle, and you are on the way to success.

It is even better if the lumps have their own flat areas, so perhaps the first operation would be to rub down the part on a sheet of abrasive on its own flat surface. Once this aspect is sorted, the clamps, too, must be carefully positioned so that they only apply pressure within the area of the triangle of contact. Should any force be applied outside this area there will be a tendency for the workpiece to tip, as pressure is inevitably going to be reduced, rather than increased, from one of the contact points as the clamp is applied and tightened. In all cases like this

Fig. 1.2 ARC 030-140-01500 Universal vice. This is not just any vice, but an accurate, solid, swivelling, tilting, universal machinists' vice. ARC EURO TRADE LTD

on and add an extra clamp or a locating block so that any movement that could lead to disaster is properly constrained. In addition, keep one ear tuned to the noise of the machine and be ready to hit the off button as soon as you detect any change.

THE SCIENCE BACKGROUND

Readers who can remember all their A-level physics can perhaps skip this bit if they wish. Others will need to understand some fairly basic science, mainly about force, friction, lubrication and leverage.

Force

Force is the scientific term for a push or a pull. Whenever metal is cut, forces are involved and it is important to understand how best to avoid any problems this might cause. Turning in a lathe involves forces on the cutting tool, usually downwards, resisted by the toolpost and its mountings, but there is an equal (and opposite) force on the workpiece, which is not so obvious as it whirls round. This whirling also causes this force on the work to vary in direction, and perhaps in size, continuously and adds new forces to the equation due to the rotation itself. It is the forces applied by the work-holding devices, and the friction this creates, that prevent the workpiece from moving in its mounting. Ideally this should rely on a positive location in the mounting, but where this is not possible we have to rely on friction alone. As this is less secure the solution is to take small cuts and take your time, so that the loads on

where contact is only on a small area, there is a risk of damage to the accurate surface of the machine, so always remember to use a flat piece of copper, or aluminium, to protect the surface and be particularly careful not to bolt down onto chips of swarf.

A further factor to consider when working out how best to hold a part is the question 'what will happen if it does start to come loose?' If it is possible

that the workpiece will be nudged in a direction that increases the load on the tooling, the work is likely to be dragged by the tool further into engagement with each revolution, leading very quickly to disaster. At the very least the tool will be snapped, the work distorted and the machine stalled. Perhaps the internal gears will be stripped of teeth and the motor burnt out. Do have this possibility in mind before you switch all the vital contact areas are reduced. In a milling operation, there are forces just the same, but this time the tool rotates quickly and the work moves slowly. The principle of positive location of the workpiece can be easier to apply in this case, as it is usually simple to attach a stop-block to the table carrying the work.

It is important to understand exactly how the force is generated by the cutting process and how this can vary, not just in the size of the force, but in its direction too, as the cut is completed, so that you can ensure that there is firm resistance at all times. When work is held in a vice, for example, the direction of the cut should always be mainly towards the fixed jaw and not away from it, or sideways. This jaw is made in one piece with the base of the vice and so is more rigid than the moving jaw, and any variation in loading against the fixed jaw is also less likely to fidget things loose. A further advantage follows when the cut is towards the fixed part of the vice, and the vice is mounted so that its operating handle is towards you the operator: the hot sharp milling swarf will tend to be thrown away from you, which is better in every way.

Another effect of force is that it always causes distortion. There is no such thing as an absolutely rigid material, so there must always be a balance between the forces needed to hold work in place and to machine it, and the results of the distortion this produces. The side pressure from the cutting tool on a bar in the lathe will bend the workpiece, distort the chuck and the mandrel that carries it, push the mandrel away in the oil film in the headstock bearings and push the headstock out of line with the bed and the tailstock. Not much, in most cases, but it happens every time. Meanwhile the tool is pushed down and back against the toolpost and all the tiny clearances that allow the tool slide to move and the cross-slide to move and the saddle to move are shoved back, putting a load on the bed, which itself then twists, ensuring that neither the tool nor the work is quite where it ought to be. All these effects are worse on a machine that is small and spindly, or old and worn or badly adjusted, with cutting tools that are not perfectly formed and a bit blunt. Much of the distortion can be accommodated by taking a second, and perhaps a third, cut with the same tool settings as the final size is approached, as with each extra pass there is much less metal to remove, and so less force and less distortion.

Reasonable precision can generally be achieved with chunky metal workpieces, sensible clamping away from any thin or delicate areas and an understanding of what is going on; thin tubes and plastics though, inevitably need special consideration. With most engineering materials the forces we need to apply do not cause permanent distortion; any flexing springs back once the forces stop. In technical terms this is because we do not exceed the 'elastic limit' of the material. Any marks left from the clamping process show that in these areas the limit has been exceeded, so where this is likely to be a problem we need to think again. The use of softer metal strips between the jaws of a bench vice is a common example of this practice; a box of light alloy or copper offcuts should always be kept handy for use whenever such a problem is likely. In this process we are relying on permanent distortion of the softer metal until the areas in contact are large enough (and the pressures low enough) to resist further distortion. Remember, though, that there are some areas of contact where the pressure cannot be reduced in this way. In particular the bearing surface of a T-nut in the slot is fixed and there is no room for soft metal inserts, so there has to be a limit on how tight you make them.

Another principle that can help you understand force and how it affects things is to consider a log lying on the ground with two ropes on the end. You pull one towards you and your mate pulls the other to him. The log will move in a direction between the two ropes, more or less to one side or the other, depending on how hard each of you is pulling. If you apply two forces to something, the 'resultant' is a single force acting between the two. The same happens in reverse too. A single force can be split into two: think about a round bar resting in a V-block, where the down force of gravity produces a side force on both sides of the block. This is a very useful principle as this can simplify the clamping process whenever you can apply a force into a corner: one clamp can fix a part in two directions at the same time.

Friction

The resistance to sideways sliding movement when two surfaces are pressed together by a force. It is friction that gives tyres their grip on the road and your fingers their grip on the side of a glass. The harder you press, the more grip there is: in scientific terms, the friction increases as the force pushing the surfaces together increases. This understanding is vital in the workshop. It is friction that holds the machinery together, it holds the tool in its holder, it stops the nuts and bolts from coming loose and, in most cases, it is the only effect we rely on for our work holding. We don't need to go into the mathematics or look at coefficients, or involved calculations, as long as the basic principle is understood.

Lubrication

Friction is reduced by lubrication, but mainly when the surfaces are already moving. Dry surfaces are always better when we need friction, although in our workshops there is no need (and usually no opportunity) to ensure clinical cleanliness of the surfaces in contact. A good wipe with a clean rag is usually enough, but sometimes it can help to use a strip of strong paper between surfaces where extra friction is needed. Steel on steel or cast iron give good results: the railways rely on this friction to drive tons of train along as well as to stop them. Most workshop metals are about as effective too, but some plastics can present problems. Materials such as PTFE (Teflon), which is used for coating non-stick pans, could be expected to be rather slippery and might need to be located more positively than by relying on friction alone. One other important factor is to be sure there are no loose particles between surfaces. If there are bits of swarf, or other debris, or sawdust

between the clamped surfaces, or burrs on the edges from previous operations, the friction (as well as the accuracy) is likely to be much lower and damage is likely. Trapped swarf is likely to embed itself in the softer surface (and sometimes the harder one too) and as a result what started as a reliable location becomes insecure and loose enough to move. Friction between clamped surfaces can be increased by interleaving paper; decorator's lining paper can be very effective. Avoid any papers that are shiny, or are embossed or printed – it is the exposed fibre of the paper that is most helpful.

In many cases the load that pushes the surfaces together is applied not directly, but using some sort of clamp (usually more than one). This is where the science of levers can be important.

Leverage

Leverage is the process by which a force in one place can be transferred to another, using a solid bar with a pivot or fulcrum to push against. This can be at one end or somewhere in the middle. A lever is also a way to change the direction of a force – changing a pull into a push or moving it through an angle. There is also a relationship to do with the length of the lever and the distance from the pivot. When you open a tin of paint, or take a tyre off a bicycle rim, you are using levers. The long end of the lever has your fairly gentle force applied and the short end turns this into a much stronger force to do the business.

Working out the best application of leverage is fairly simple. Think about

a plank resting centrally across two boxes. If you stand in the middle of the plank, your weight is carried equally by each box, because the lengths each side are equal. Move so that you are two-thirds of the way along the plank and the weight carried by the nearer box becomes twice that on the far one; the distances are in the ratio two to one, so the forces are in the same ratio. This understanding is going to be important when ensuring that you get the greatest force on the workpiece (to hold it firm) with the least force on the equipment (to avoid damage).

Vibration

Before we leave the science background it will help to look briefly at vibration. Rotating parts do not always cause vibration, but too often this cannot be ignored. It all depends on the position of the 'centre of gravity' of the rotating assembly. If its mass is centred exactly in the middle, all will be well, but in practice this is difficult to achieve. The easy way to move the centre of gravity without moving the workpiece is to add extra mass on the lighter side, and this is generally needed whenever turning is to be carried out on an offset part, such as a locomotive driving wheel with its built-in, out-of-balance segment. The effect is worse if the mounting of the machine is not properly stiff. If the machine can shake on the bench, or the whole bench can shake on the floor, there will be speeds at which even a minor out-of-balance can send the whole affair into a wild rhythm. Another cause of vibration is a mismatch between the capability of your machine and the particular set-up at the time: in other words, trying to do too much. Flexibility in the machinery can also lead to vibrations that are nothing to do with out-of-centre masses. The result shows as an odd noise, accompanied by a wavy or chequered pattern in the finished turning as the tool digs in and then springs back repeatedly. The solution to try first, and usually the easiest, whatever the cause is thought to be, is to change the speed of rotation. What you need to avoid is what is called 'resonance', the effect in which the shaking is at the same frequency of rotation or an exact multiple of its frequency. The effect can sometimes cause odd noises elsewhere in the workshop, as some unconnected part starts to rattle in sympathy with the speed of your rotating parts. Speeding up or slowing down, even by a small amount, can help to keep any vibration effects within sensible bounds, otherwise the answer might be to carry through this troublesome operation so slowly, or to limit the depth of cut, that the vibration does not amount to a problem.

MEASUREMENTS

A few words about measurements – the UK has been trying to get to grips with the metric system for many years, and many of our readers will have been educated almost entirely with metric units. Accordingly, we will use the metric system too, but that won't stop the occasional reference to 'an inch or two', just for old time's sake. My advice to anyone who still has difficulty with the metric system, or indeed with old-fashioned inches and sixteenths, is to equip yourself with some electronic aids, a calculator and a digital calliper at least. The calliper will change metric dimensions to imperial in an instant as you measure and the calculator will help in turning fractions of an inch into something that any modern schoolboy can understand. In any case, although super precision is a requirement for some model making or similar tasks, most of the tools you might need for work holding itself do not need precise dimensions or super-flat surfaces. Some do though, and some need accurate angles too, but always remember that the accuracy you get is limited by the inherent precision of your machines, your measuring equipment and the rest of your workshop. Certainly it is possible to achieve very precise work, but only with very expensive tooling, a long and costly training period and even then in a controlled environment where the temperature in particular is held steady.

FINISH

Because the amateur machinist tends to be working to produce one or two parts of a given design, and rarely more than three or four identical parts, many machining jobs can take much longer in the setting up and finishing than in the cutting of metal. This is inevitable, but one additional reason for jobs to take a long time relates to a tradition among machining publications, and their writers, that only work of exhibition standard should be illustrated. Writers of the old school, who went through an old-fashioned apprenticeship, are naturally very proud of their skills and their superbly equipped workshops and they do not want to lower their standards. This is reflected in their writing as well as in their worked examples and has naturally led beginners to try to achieve the same high standards from the start, even for parts that will never leave the workshop. This, in turn, has led to frustration in those who are not yet so accomplished or so well kitted out.

The real world, though, does not have to be like that. Of course, the driving wheels of a model locomotive really do need to be round and the same diameter, and their axle bores concentric, not just because that looks right, but because without this accuracy the finished product will not work properly. But if you are making a clamp or a bracket for your own workshop use, it really matters a lot less if the holes are not exactly in line or the edges machined all over and then draw-filed to perfection, as long as the finished part performs the function intended. Do not be disheartened if your early efforts do not display the craftsmanship that will come with practice. At the same time though, you should learn from each task, note any imperfections, and consider how you might do better next time.

Among the things that do matter for every job, and not merely for appearance, is the finish of the edges and corners. All machining can leave a 'burr' on the edges, especially along the trailing edge of the cut, and these burrs can cause serious problems. They can prevent the work from sitting properly against the locating fixtures, they can put permanent bruises on the surfaces of your machine and they can cut your fingers to ribbons. It is simple and quick, to use a 'smooth' file to remove any burrs or sharp edges and corners after each operation is completed, producing a small chamfer on each of the edges. Do the same with any holes, using a big drill bit or a countersink. One of the handiest tools alongside my pillar drill is a small rechargeable screwdriver fitted with a countersink bit.

2 Workholding on Lathe and Milling Machine

What follows may seem to be set out in a rather odd order, but I have tried to achieve a logical flow from the relatively simple in practice to the more complicated. As the lathe is the first machine tool many of us acquire, and as the lathe comes ready fitted, almost always, with a three-jaw chuck, that is where we will start.

THREE- AND FOUR-JAW SCROLL CHUCKS

The most common way to hold your work for turning is in a chuck, especially if the work is round or nearly so. Chucks come in a range of sizes and designs, all of them ideal for some jobs but not so good for others. For turning short work of moderate diameter, the three-jaw chuck can be used on its own. Simply adjust the jaws to size, position a short piece of bar between them as far as it will go, tighten the jaws and that is the work-holding part of the job complete. The T-shaped chuck key is all you need for this, and you should never use an extension or other means to increase the leverage; this is likely to cause permanent damage to the internals of the chuck. Perhaps the work will not be held as accurately central as could be, but it would be perfectly adequate for making a thick washer or spacer, or similar simple part. If the component is rather larger in diameter, up to the diameter of the chuck itself, the jaws can be replaced by an alternative set, or reversed in their slots, depending on the exact design.

For many jobs though, when the bar to be machined is more than an inch or two long, and particularly when it is a small diameter, a chuck is not relied upon as the only support as there needs to be further support away from the chuck end. In such cases, the lathe tailstock is fitted with a conical-pointed 'centre', which locates in a small conical hole in the end of the work away from the chuck. The centre is located in an accurate slightly tapered hole (almost always a 'Morse Taper', MT) in the tailstock, it is important when fitting it to ensure that its surface, and that of the hole, is clean. Any debris that is allowed to remain will ensure that the work is neither accurately where it should be, nor held firmly. Apply a little grease (ordinary wheel bearing or high melting point grease will do fine) to the point of the centre, and this will lubricate the rubbing surface of the workpiece. Then tighten the tailstock point (not too firmly) into the hole in the work. This extra support helps in two major ways: it resists the tendency for the turning forces to distort the workpiece and it stops the work from fidgeting out through the chuck as work proceeds. If you have a long session of turning in mind, you might use a 'live centre', which has the same taper fitting

Morse Tapers – common sizes				
		MT1	MT2	MT3
Taper per foot	(in)	0.59858	0.59941	0.60235
Small end	(in)	0.369	0.572	0.778
	(mm)	9.37	14.53	19.76
Large end	(in)	0.475	0.700	0.938
	(mm)	12.07	17.78	23.83

but with bearings inside so that the tip rotates with the work. These are more expensive and a bit bulkier, but they do avoid any potential for overheating and expansion or wear through friction. If you do continue with a plain centre, check from time to time that the tailstock is neither too tight, nor slightly loose, as both the machine and the workpiece will warm up and expand, and at different rates, during machining.

Where it is not possible to use a centre hole in the work, use can be made of an extra chuck mounted on a 'rolling tailstock' on which it can spin; the chuck holds firmly on to the work and turns with it, supported in the taper in the tailstock. This is not likely to be an operation you will need to do very often, so perhaps you can delay this purchase until it is really useful. The headstock or driving end of the lathe is also able to carry a centre, and we will be looking at this in due course, for some operations where a chuck is not used at all.

Another method of supporting the outer end of long work held in the chuck is a 'steady' (for details see Chapter 4).

Every chuck drives the work by friction, and this needs a force applied to each of the contact surfaces; this is what happens as you tighten the chuck key and a scroll or thread within the chuck moves each jaw in or out. The forces involved can create two problems, one for the chuck and the other for the work itself. If the workpiece is short and does not extend back into the body of the chuck, all the force holding the work is acting at the outer ends of the jaws, this tends to tilt and perhaps

to strain them and the scroll inside the chuck. To counteract this, a separate metal ring should be used at the inside of the chuck, perhaps made from scrap, turned in advance to the same diameter as the work, so that when the chuck key is tightened the jaws bear equally on the work and the spare ring, preventing any tendency to bell-mouth the jaws, and maintaining the firm hold of the chuck. If the workpiece is thin, a tube for example, it may not be possible to tighten the chuck without seriously distorting the work. In this case an extra piece should be made, again from scrap, fitting inside the tube, so that it will resist the pressure of the jaws; or of course, fitting around the tube, if you are relying on the jaws moving outwards for grip. Another way to ensure that the work does not move is to hold it firmly endways in the chuck with a draw-bolt passing right through the live spindle. A length of high-tensile studding (or all-thread) is handy for this, with a thick washer and nut at both ends.

Now a word of warning for those of you who have a lathe on which the chuck is screwed onto the mandrel, as many small lathes do. In normal turning operations the chuck rotates so that the top moves towards you, the forces from the cutting process tend to tighten the chuck onto its mounting. Turning processes are usually done this way round for this reason, but sometimes a chuck is used to hold parts in place on other tooling, such as a rotary table, or for other operations. The forces from these operations need always to be arranged so that the tendency is to tighten the chuck. If this is not done and the chuck starts to come undone, it can rapidly

lead to a jam in which the workpiece (the tool, the holding tools and the drive system) can all be damaged. With a full-sized industrial lathe the chuck is locked in place, often with a system of pegs, so the chuck can be driven in either direction. This does not remove the risk entirely though, as such workshops are often equipped with other work-holding tools, such as dividing heads, which do rely on screw-fitted chucks.

Three-jaw chucks, self-centring

This is the most common chuck supplied with a home machinist's lathe, or indeed with a big one. Three-jaw chucks are also used fitted to rotary tables and dividing heads and whenever a rigid yet adjustable holder for round (or hexagonal) work is required.

Turn the chuck key (or for some small chucks, the tommy-bar) and the three jaws move in, or out, together, so that they grip a cylindrical (or hexagonal) part and hold it fairly central, as long as there is no out-of-square or taper on the locating surfaces. Holding tapered parts is more complex and will be covered later. The chuck jaws will also grip inside a cylindrical recess or through the hole by expanding outwards, while the surfaces of the jaws that face towards the tailstock are ground flat so that a ring or flange will sit square against them. Most versions of this type of chuck come with a set of extra jaws with steps the other way round, so that they can hold larger work on the outside. To change the jaw set, turn the chuck key (or tommy-bar) to move the jaws fully outwards and

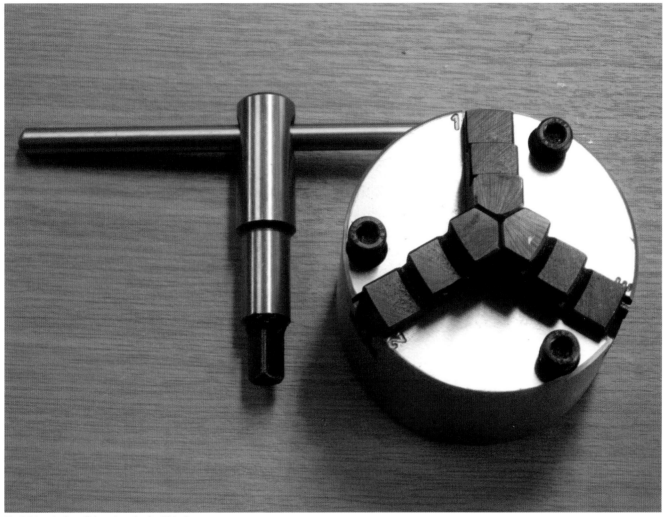

Fig. 2.1 A typical small three-jaw chuck with its key.

collect them as they are freed from their slots. Note that the jaws and the slots are numbered, you need to fit the alternatives in their correct slots in number order or they won't meet in the middle. To avoid mistakes, turn the chuck key before adding the jaws and watch for the start of the scroll-thread as it moves in the number one slot, then back off slightly and add the jaw as you turn the key slowly. Then do the same for the remaining jaws and slots in order.

You should remember, however,

that the centring of this type of chuck is not always very good. This is because of the way the jaws are operated. The back of each jaw carries teeth rather like a slice of a coarse thread, these teeth engage with a scroll that is rotated by the chuck key. In small chucks the scroll is machined on the knurled ring, which has holes for the tommy-bar, but the principle is the same exactly. The scroll needs clearance in its housing, introducing an error in centralizing, and on top of this, the scroll itself is subject to

distortion and wear, especially at the jaw positions most commonly used in practice. Do not put a round bar in the chuck and expect it to run true, or rely on being able to take out a circular part and put it back so it runs true. The error won't be very much, especially with a new lathe and a quality chuck. Unless you are seeking perfection, you may find that you get acceptable repeatability if you mark on the workpiece to align with an identified jaw, so that once turning has started you can stop, remove and replace the work without disturbing the concentricity too much.

If you really need concentric accuracy, and you only have the one chuck, it is possible to measure the eccentricity when the chuck is tight on the work, using a Dial Test Indicator (DTI), and to add thin packing between the jaw and the work to correct any error. Set the work up with the DTI point resting on top of the surface to be machined, turn the work slowly by hand and note the amount and position of the highest

place. Slacken the chuck slightly, select a strip of shim of half the out-of-round dimension and slide it under the jaw nearest to the top. Be sure to use a narrow strip, with no sharp edges likely to catch on anything, especially not on you. Take the readings again in the same way. It might take two or three attempts to get the shimming exactly right. Remember though, that this is a 'last resort' method, it will take some time to perfect and you should not expect to take a heavy or intermittent

cut without problems.

Another possibility depends on how your chuck is mounted to the headstock spindle. Some small chucks, especially those supplied as part of a complete small lathe outfit, are held on the mandrel by a thread in the one-piece chuck body, in which case you are stuck, but with luck your chuck will be bolted to a separate threaded backplate. This means that the chuck could perhaps be moved slightly on the backplate until the work runs true

Fig. 2.2 Checking for concentricity using a DTI on a magnetic stand.

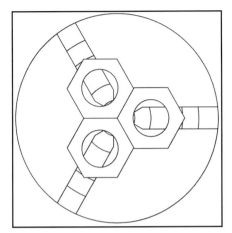

Fig. 2.3 The nuts slipped over the chuck jaws to hold very small drills.

(even though this will put the chuck itself eccentric). For this to be a simple operation, there needs to be a smaller than standard diameter for the locating shoulder (called the 'register') on the backplate, this will allow the

location of the chuck to be varied, but it also makes it harder to re-centralize the chuck again ready for other jobs, so ideally you need two backplates so that one can be turned down a millimetre or so to give this flexibility when it is vital, while the other remains unmodified. Another option is to machine matching recesses in chuck and backplate, and to make up a register ring (like a big thick washer) to locate between them. Two such rings need to be made, one fitting both sides properly, for use when the chuck needs to be central and one with a modest clearance (perhaps a millimetre) so that the chuck can be offset to compensate for wear, or irregular bar, and similar concerns. Further solutions are available, using an independent-jaw chuck for example (see later), but an extra backplate is going to be cheaper and simpler than an extra chuck, and

a couple of register rings cheaper still. One problem you might find with the eccentric chuck method is out-of-balance vibration at high speeds. Unless the chuck has been moved a lot more than a millimetre out of centre, this is not likely to be a disaster, but do start the lathe gradually and if vibration is a problem, do the machining at a lower speed.

As each chuck jaw has a hollow radius ground on its inner surface, to grip smoothly on the work without marking it, the chuck cannot close completely so it is not possible to hold a very small bar or drill bit in the chuck. To get round this, one dodge is to use three hexagons, each bored with an accurately central hole, one mounted on the end of each jaw. Use steel nuts bored out to fit over the jaw tips and choose precision nuts turned from

Fig. 2.4 The sharp edges on the bar-turned nut, compared with a pressed version.

sharp-edged hexagon bar, rather than mass-produced pressed nuts, which have rounded corners. Alternatively, you can use the chuck jaws to hold a small drill chuck mounted on its own cylindrical spindle. With very small work though, the lack of concentricity can become more serious and a better bet would be to use a more accurate type of holder, such as a collet (for examples see Chapter 3).

Four-jaw chucks, independent

In this type of chuck each jaw has its own adjustment, so there is no attempt to make centring automatic: instead of a scroll there are four coarse-thread spindles. This means that you can hold most irregular shapes securely and, with a bit of patience, centre your work exactly before you start to turn. If there is a cylindrical surface that needs to be accurately central, a DTI can be applied directly to measure, and help correct, any eccentricity. Otherwise, use a centre punch to mark on the job the exact centre you need for the machining operation. If this is to become a hole in due course, use a centre drill to make the mark even clearer. Set the work up in the approximate position by eye, tightening each jaw in turn (but not too tight at this stage). Turn the lathe spindle slowly by hand, note how the centre mark is not truly central, and position the chuck so that the position of your centre mark is offset horizontally

Fig. 2.5 With four jaws adjusted independently, this chuck is more versatile than a three-jaw version, but more fiddly to set up.

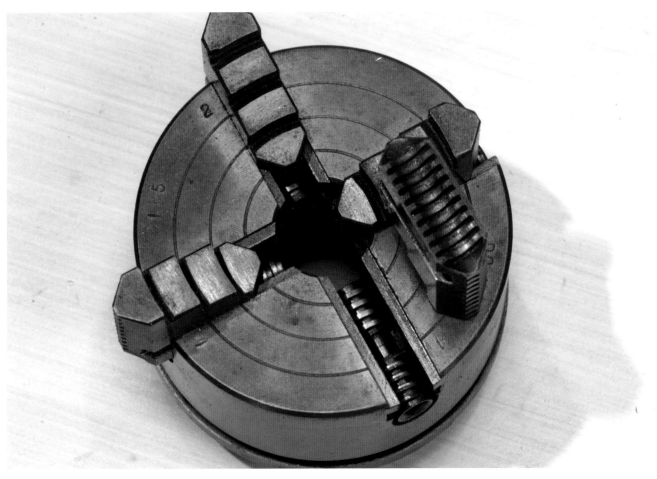

Fig. 2.6 With one jaw removed, the coarse-thread that moves it in and out can be seen.

away from you. The toolpost can be fitted with a pointer and adjusted to act as a guide for this operation or you can use an unworn centre in the tailstock. Slacken the opposite chuck jaw on your side slightly, rotate the chuck through half a turn and tighten the opposite jaw. Try the centring again, and hope that you have improved matters. Go through the same routine again, positioning the offset centre away from you, and adjusting the horizontal pair of jaws in turn. It will take a bit of practice before this centring becomes an easy operation, as the jaw threads

are always rather coarse, for strength. Sometimes it only needs the merest nudge or even less on the handle of the chuck key. There is no point in thinking of shim packing for this job, as with care the jaws can always be adjusted to centre the work properly. That said, it is sometimes helpful for delicate or nearly finished parts to use a strip of paper packing on every chuck jaw when you start, to reduce the chance of marking the work.

Before you turn the power on, tighten each jaw by exactly the same amount so the work is firmly held and,

with the lathe out of gear, spin the spindle with one hand to see if it is in balance, or tends to settle always in the same place. This is likely if the workpiece is heavier at one side than another. If this is the case, you have two options. You can perhaps add a weight to the light side, if there is a secure way to attach it, adjusting the weight until the spindle shows no inclination to stop in a particular position. The change-gears supplied with the lathe are often used for this balancing role as the various sizes are, of course, varying masses. If this cannot be done, set the lathe to a

Fig. 2.7 *Using a wobbler to correct eccentric running of a centre pop.*

low speed for the turning operation. In any case, only proceed if the lathe is firmly bolted to a rigid bench, which itself is firmly fixed to the wall or the floor. Running at normal turning speed with an out-of-balance load can cause the whole set-up to shake very badly. If your spindle cannot be turned without the motor turning, so that you cannot check for balance, engage a low speed and take up the drive gently, be prepared to stop everything at once if the shakes begin to develop.

For greater accuracy in centring the work, make use of a DTI, which should be arranged to bear on a true cylindrical part of the work. As you turn the chuck by hand, the DTI's pointer will give a very accurate indication, not only where the high or low positions are but by how much they run eccentric. If you only have a centre-punch mark or a small centre bore as a guide, rather than an accurate cylindrical surface, a 'wobbler' can be carried in the toolpost or the tailstock. This comprises a short ball-ended bar located in its own miniature spherical chuck. The outer end of the bar can be another small sphere or a pointer. Move the wobbler so the outer ball-end rests in the centre, or the pointed end rests in the centre

pop, and watch as you turn the chuck by hand. If the centre mark on the work is adjusted to be truly central, no movement of the wobbler will be seen. When the wobbler is drawn out a small distance and the chuck turned halfway, the end will fit exactly into the centre again without any tendency to jump sideways. If it does move, then the centring is not yet perfect.

Of course, there are times when the need is to set work deliberately off-centre, this is where an independent chuck scores again over the scroll type. A component named because it is made off-centre comes to mind immediately, the eccentric used to operate the valve-gear of many steam engines. A slice of round bar can be mounted in an independent chuck with confidence and the required offset checked using a DTI on the bar itself or, if it is a thin slice and not as deep as the jaws extend, on the insides of the jaws. Although the jaws are ground to a radius on the inside holding surface, with work offset in this way this radius will not bear properly on the two 'sides' of the eccentric, and as the outer face of the eccentric is likely to have been finished to size as a bearing surface, thin strips of copper or brass should be used where the 'side' jaws touch. The other two jaws, those nearest the centre and furthest from the centre of the chuck in this case, will bear centrally on the work, with the radius aligned properly and the two jaws between them at the same equal setting, so that the dimensions for the offset can be read easily.

Chucks like these with independent jaw operation are not supplied with alternative inside-out jaws; instead, the jaws can be removed and turned round so that the steps are reversed. Sometimes it is handy to do this with one or two jaws without at the same time reversing the others, for example when you need to accommodate work that is much longer than it is wide or where the section to be turned is not concentric with the locating surfaces. A job where this can be very useful is the outer component of the steam engine eccentric mentioned above, called the strap, which needs to be bored in the lathe to fit the eccentric itself and is mainly circular around the outer circumference, but with flats where the

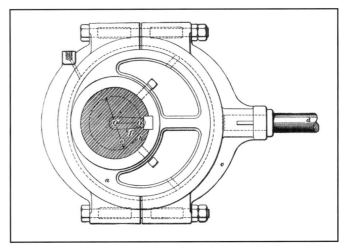

Fig. 2.8 A steam engine eccentric from a 1907 drawing.

two halves bolt together, and a bulge where the driving rod will be fixed.

Four-jaw chucks, self-centring

These are not as broadly useful perhaps, as either of the chucks already covered, but very handy if much of your turning involves square stock and you need a quick set-up without centring each job individually. The principle of self-centring is the same as on the three-jaw version, with an internal scroll and with inside and outside jaw sets. One difficulty with this design arises when the workpiece is not exactly square. In such cases, only two jaws will tighten properly on the work, which can then fidget about as the cutting loads are applied. You might even come across six-jaw chucks, intended for special applications such as cutter grinding machines, but useful just the same for other jobs, although the same concerns can apply if the work is not exactly round or symmetrically hexagonal.

JAWS FOR CHUCKS

One further option for some (but not all) self-centring chucks is the availability of soft jaws. These do not have the steps found on standard jaws, but because they are not hardened they can be machined with your own steps or other profiles to suit any job that might be difficult to hold in the standard jaws. For example, they could be used to make washers of special sizes from standard versions, using the jaws modified with a notch to hold the outer washer diameter for boring the centres and then locating in the new central hole to turn the outsides. Doing this machining yourself on your machine is a good way to ensure concentricity. An alternative design of chuck is made (but only, it seems, for large lathes or for wood turners) with jaws that come in two parts: a threaded or toothed inner section that is moved by the chuck key as normally, with an outer face onto which separate jaws can be bolted. A range of extra bolt-on jaws is available, some of which could readily be modified to suit relatively lightweight metal machining tasks. Whenever you decide to modify soft jaws of any type, tighten them in the chuck onto a spare length of accurate bar or inside an accurate ring, such as a bearing race, before machining starts. This will hold them firm and make the machining more precise. Ideally, set the jaws as far open as they will be in use, as this should result in better concentricity. Soft jaws are not generally available (or necessary) for independent chucks, as their jaws work perfectly well inside out.

THINKING OF BUYING AN EXTRA CHUCK?

Here are a few things you might like to consider:

◆ Before you splash out, read through the rest of this volume and consider whether any of the alternative methods or tools might serve your needs better – at least for the time being. It is true that you really cannot have too large a selection of chucks, but even then there are going to be jobs that you cannot manage to hold effectively without tools of a different type.

◆ Measure carefully the space for the chuck on your lathe, and note the exact sizes of tapers and threads. Any new tooling will be useless if it is not compatible or simply won't fit.

◆ Think carefully about any other extras you already have or might need, such as a rotary table, and ensure that any chuck you add to your kit can be used with this additional equipment.

◆ Be very wary of second-hand chucks, especially in the hobby or home workshop sizes. Inevitably these tools may have been mishandled by their often amateur users, and in the smaller or cheaper models there is less strength and less accuracy to start with. You need a good opportunity to examine what is offered, including a check for accuracy when mounted on its spindle and with the jaws in a range of positions, before taking the plunge.

◆ You might find an extra drill chuck handy, fitted to a taper to match your lathe and mill. Two types of chuck are generally available, those that are tightened by hand and those that have their own small chuck key. The keyless type is common on electric drills: professional all-metal examples are usually more accurate, though more expensive, and very useful for starting accurate holes with a small centre. Rohm Supra and Albrecht are favourite names. Rotation in the conventional right-handed sense tends to tighten the hold, but in reverse the opposite can happen. This makes this type of chuck hopeless for holding a tap and similar jobs that rely on turning both ways alternately. The chuck-key type (often called a Jacobs Chuck from a favourite maker) is much better in this regard, holding firm in both directions, but never so accurately central in use.

3   Collets and Collet Chucks

For many turning jobs, a more accurate and repeatable method to hold cylindrical work involves the use of a collet, usually located in a special holder. Collets are hardened steel sleeves, usually with a taper on the outside and an accurately concentric cylindrical hole in the middle, and slotted lengthwise so that they can be contracted slightly. This design ensures that the collets can be ground to accurate dimensions with large contacting surfaces, so that they remain concentric in use. This concentricity means that you can swap cylindrical parts, or collets, from one machine to another with repeatable precision, with the further advantage of contact with the holding tool over almost the whole surface, rather than over three or four narrow strips. Should a collet be strained or otherwise damaged, a new collet is also much cheaper than a new chuck. We will explain what is generally available first and then go on to their uses.

The simplest collets are made to fit into the taper of a headstock (or tailstock), pulled into place and contracted by tightening a threaded drawbar passing right through the spindle. The sizes are limited by the size of the taper and this depends on the machine you have. Very small lathes may not have a headstock taper at all, but mostly they are MT2 (taking collets 2mm to 12mm)

Fig. 3.1 These Morse Taper collets fit within the taper in the headstock or tailstock. They can be drawn tight using a drawbar.

or MT3 (3mm to 18mm), with corresponding inch sizes also available. With all collets that rely on a taper, as the collet is contracted around the work, its outer surface ceases to be an exact cone, this limits the amount of contraction that is allowed, so normally a range of collets is supplied in 1mm steps. The drawbar thread in the collet has two versions, metric and inch, and needs to match the drawbar thread you have available (or what comes with your lathe or mill). One complication is that in the popular MT2 size the options are ⅜in Whitworth or M10 × 1.5mm. The Whitworth thread will screw into an M10 hole for two or three turns and then tends to jam. This

can damage both parts, so try to stick to all Whitworth or all M10 for this role. Generally a modern machine will have metric threads throughout as standard, but alternatives exist, so be careful with any additions to your kit.

To remove an MT collet, slacken the drawbar by a turn or two, and tap the outer end (furthest from the collet itself) smartly towards the collet with a copper hammer. This should loosen the collet so that it can be unscrewed and removed completely. This procedure is not ideal though, as the sudden shock load is not good for the headstock bearings. If your lathe has a captive drawbar (as more commonly fitted to milling

Fig. 3.2 A selection of ER collet holders, closing nuts and C-spanner.

machines), it will only be necessary to continue turning the drawbar after the first loosening; you will find that it then goes tight again as the collet is ejected automatically. If not, and you find it difficult to free your Morse Taper fittings, then perhaps you need to reconsider how tight you are pulling up the drawbar. The taper itself is capable of providing the friction without over-tightening; the drawbar is there to eliminate any tendency for the fitting to fidget loose as work proceeds.

For another way to avoid having to employ some form of impact to remove these collets or the tools they carry, as well as to hold a more useful range of tool and bar sizes, alternative designs of collets can be used, fitting into their own more steeply tapered holders. The most widely available system in home workshop sizes is called ER. These collets come in a range of basic sizes and a variety of holders are made to fit the standard Morse Tapers (MT), using the standard drawbar system, and for use on a chuck backplate and in stand-alone holders. Because they rely on a collet holder rather than having to fit within the spindle taper, they can cover a larger range of sizes. (As examples, the MT2 version takes ER25 collets from 1mm to 16mm, MT3 takes ER32 from 1mm to 20mm.) The actual collets are tapered at both ends and are closed with a threaded lock ring, using a special spanner. For jobs where the grip needs to be very tight, such as cutting a thread with a die, special ball-bearing lock rings can be used. Where no taper is available in the head-stock or rotary table, flange-mounted holders are also made to fit on a stand-ard chuck backplate or faceplate, or to bolt directly to a rotary table for milling jobs. It can sometimes be handy to use this flange type of fitting on a machine even though it has a taper mandrel too, as this will allow the use of longer stock passing right through the collet into the mandrel, an option not possible with ER holders made to fit Morse Tapers. There are also collet holders with a parallel shank designed to be held in a chuck, ideal for anyone without an MT taper in the spindle or whose taper has been irrevocably damaged (by a previous owner, of course).

The ER range of collets is the most useful for the home machinist with limited resources, in my view, as they can be used whether or not there is a machine taper. They can be used to hold milling cutters as well as round workpieces, they have a wider range of sizes than collets fitting directly into a Morse Taper, changing sizes and tools is quick and easy, and their accuracy and repeatability are excellent. Because the tapers involved are not so gradual, ER collets do not (usually) require an impact to loosen them. The collet nut itself has an internal flange that fits in a groove in the collet and releases it automatically as the nut is loosened. This groove arrangement has sometimes caused problems for beginners, who perhaps do not realize that each collet needs to be clicked into the collet nut before it is fitted into the holder.

Some larger lathes and mills do not have a Morse Taper in the mandrel, but are made with a parallel bore with a taper at the outer end. The taper is rather steeper than the Morse version, but otherwise works in a similar way. This is the R8 system and, of course, you need R8 collets to fit: there is a wide range of sizes available, up to ⅞in or 18mm. Just like Morse Collets, the R8 closing process relies on a drawbar, this time with a ⁷⁄₁₆in UNF thread. Whereas MT and ER collets are readily available only with cylindrical holes; the R8 series

Fig. 3.3 ER collets are the most useful, but only for circular parts.

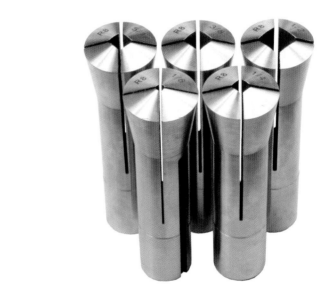
Fig. 3.4 All collet systems rely on conical locating surfaces. These special square-hole versions are called R8. ARC EURO TRADE LTD

Fig. 3.5 Another collet system, C5, includes collets with a variety of hole shapes; these are hexagonal. ARC EURO TRADE LTD

includes a range of squares too.

If you need hexagonal holes to hold a more specialized bar, the 5C collet system is the only readily available option at home workshop sizes (and then, only for even larger machines as these collets themselves are fairly chunky). There is again a range of holders, fitting onto standard lathe or rotary table backplates, and special holding fixtures for milling or grinding work. In the 5C version, as in the R8, the collets are cylindrical over much of their outer diameter, slotted lengthwise, with a thread at the inner end, and an outwards taper at the other. The thread is used to pull the collet into the fixture; this pulls the collet into the taper, closing it onto the work. Round sizes go up to 28mm, and the square and hexagonal to 19mm or ¾in. There are also 5C step collets on sale with large plain outer ends in unhardened steel, so you can turn a recess to match the outside of any special washer or flange, and 5C expanding collets in a range of sizes to grip parts precisely by locating inside an accurate bore.

A search of the catalogues and the Web will reveal a further range of collet systems, some for specialized trades like clock or pen making, others designed specifically for a particular make of machine, but those detailed here have been selected as they are widely available in useful sizes and at fairly sensible prices. Before deciding to add any of these clever devices to your lathe equipment, you really need to think hard about your needs, now and for the future. If your grandfather has left you a cabinet full of 5C collets that might make your decision easier, of course, especially if you get the machine to go with them. Otherwise you need to look at your ambitions, to add an extra machine perhaps, and make sure that whatever you acquire is as universally useful as possible. A further factor is the long-term availability of replacement parts. Chose a standard regularly catalogued version and it is more likely that in five year's time, when you need a couple of extra sizes, they will still be available.

4   Turning Between Centres

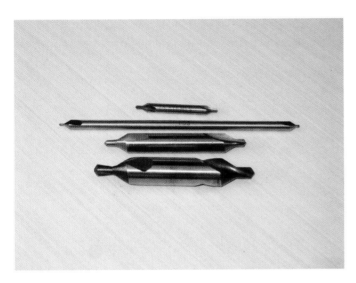

Fig. 4.1 Centre drills are used to make the 60-degree locations in which a centre locates. Special long versions help to clear obstructions, such as holding clamps.

This method of work holding goes right back to the days of woodland bodgers, making chair legs and ladder rungs on pole lathes, without anything fancy like a chuck or collet. It remains a useful technique though, and can be used for jobs that are very difficult by more up-to-the-minute methods. In brief, the work is held between two steel points called 'centres', locating in countersunk holes drilled for the purpose in each end of the job (also called centres, just to keep you on your toes). The drive is transmitted to the work by a peg on the lathe backplate, driving a clamp fixed around the work. This method of turning is a favourite for checking the accuracy and alignment of a lathe, as there is no reliance on fancy extra parts that themselves might not be

accurate. The method involves turning a diameter at each end of a long bar using the same tool settings and measuring the diameters produced. To avoid turning the whole length of bar in this process, the central section is relieved by turning it slightly smaller in advance, then the ends are turned

to size without changing the tool settings. Any variation in the diameters produced shows that something is wrong, perhaps because the bed is twisted, which could be from fitting it to a surface that is not properly flat or rigid for example, or the tailstock is offset. This is a clue to one major use of this method of holding work in metal-turning terms. By offsetting the tailstock but leaving other adjustments untouched, you can produce a tapered bar. How much taper depends on how much offset you give; as long as your cutting tool is set reasonably level with the spindle centres, and you keep the centres tight, a good taper will result. You will find on many working drawings that a taper is dimensioned as so many fractions of an inch to a foot, with no mention of degrees at all. This made the job of the toolsetter easier, as the required offset of the tailstock could

Fig. 4.2 Turning between centres, certainly the oldest and still a well-regarded method to produce accurate work.

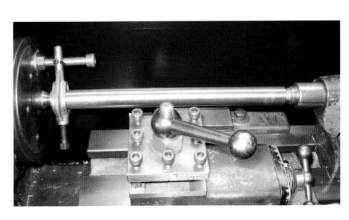

be calculated and checked fairly simply from these figures.

The work for taper turning is usually driven by a peg fitted to the headstock, perhaps a bolt fixed between nuts and washers in a slot in a faceplate. This turns a clamp called a 'dog' or 'carrier', which is fitted around the headstock end of the work. To avoid the risk of the dog turning on the workpiece in use, perhaps damaging it, file a flat on the work and to keep the drive peg from clattering it can be fixed to the arm of the dog with a cable tie or a few turns of wire. If you do not have a dog, it is possible to make an alternative from a couple of lengths of drilled bar and two bolts, or made up using a U-bolt type exhaust clamp. Remember though, that whatever you use is going to be whirling round at that end of the work, so round off any corners and be careful to keep fingers, clothing and tools away from this area.

A further use for this method of rotating a long bar is detailed later when we deal with boring bars.

Tapered parts, such as a Morse Taper fitting with a soft end that can be machined to take your workpiece, are not always easy to mount in a chuck or collet. They can, however, be held, and also produced from plain bar, by turning between centres. In fact, many commercial tapered parts are made, or finished, in this way and will often be found to have centre drillings in both ends. The difficulty of attaching a driving dog to such a part, if a locating flat would spoil the part for other purposes, can be overcome by making a tapered sleeve to match the component. This extra part will be pressed into place on the taper and will carry the drive dog, so it does not need to be much longer than a couple of centimetres and can be made from a bar-end, or a thick-walled length of tube about 25mm long, held in a chuck. The concentricity of the inner taper and the outside of the sleeve is not critical here, so a three-jaw chuck can be used without extra care about centring things. The short taper boring can be done by offsetting the tool holder slide to the correct angle, with the taper tried for a fit with the workpiece itself before removing it from the chuck. When you are happy that the taper will fit without any rocking, remove the fitting from the chuck and file, or grind, a flat on the outside surface to hold the dog. Knock the fitting firmly into place on the work, the action of tightening the dog should hold everything together for further operations.

Another way to hold tapered parts depends on the details of the taper. If you are faced with a Morse Taper that is not the size for your lathe spindle, you can use an adaptor known as a step-up sleeve or a reducing sleeve, with one end to fit your lathe and the other to fit the intended workpiece. If this is not possible, an internal taper can be carried on an external taper made to fit from round bar, carried in a collet or in a four-jaw chuck. The next section deals with the creation of external tapers. A carrier for a workpiece with an external taper may be made by a boring operation using a cross-slide set at the appropriate angle. Alternatively, if the part has a matching female part, such as a pulley for an armature, use can be made of the pulley, held in a four-jaw chuck, as a holding method. This is especially useful if there is also an extension with a thread so that the taper can be pulled up firmly. In other cases, it may be best to make up, in addition, a male taper with the same dimensions as the proposed workpiece. Then turn up a length of round bar and bore out the female taper within it to make a carrier and use the male taper as a mandrel to turn the outside of the carrier concentric and truly cylindrical, so that it can be used to carry the workpiece in a chuck.

CREATING TAPERS IN THE LATHE

One way to produce a taper relies on a toolpost made in two layers, the cross-slide (moving at right angles to the lathe axis) carrying a separate toolpost slide that can be clamped down in a range of angular positions. If turning is carried out by moving the tool with the tool holder control (and not the main feed or cross-slide) a tapered surface can be produced. Many lathes, except the very smallest, are so equipped and the main limitation with this method, which can produce internal as well as external tapers, is the relatively short tool movement possible. Turning between centres that are not in line, as is often necessary when making a longer tapered part, can be carried out using a special attachment or by offsetting the centre at the tailstock end. Such turning is not a common operation for most of us, so it may not be worth buying, or making, a special taper-turning attachment for your lathe. These rely on mounting the workpiece between centres in the normal way (that is, with centres in line not offset) and disconnecting the cross-slide adjuster mechanism, connecting the slide instead to an arm carried on a fixture running alongside the bed. The fixture is carried on an adjustable guide that will move the tool in the Y direction as the saddle moves along the bed, producing the taper as it goes.

It is worth noting here that these devices should be set up to produce a taper with the larger end towards the headstock. This is where the driving dog needs to fit, and with nothing getting in the way at the smaller end it is easy to back off the tailstock and try a mating tapered sleeve for fit. It is also necessary to turn from right to left, so that the tool is pushed away from the work as it travels along. Doing it this way means that on the return pass the slack in the system as the tool is pulled back leaves a small clearance and no cutting takes place. These points might seem obvious once you look closely at what is going on, but they are not at all obvious to every user until they get well into the process the wrong way round. Strictly speaking, neither the angled toolpost method nor the special taper-turning attachment method involves a change in conventional work-holding methods, so they are both mentioned here as background to what follows.

Neither of these methods nor the next though, can be relied upon to produce exactly the taper you need at the first pass of the tool. To be of any value as a holding device, the taper does need to be a precise fit, so it is usually necessary to try your first attempt in the matching part and to adjust the settings as needed to correct looseness at one end or the other. The fit of a taper that is nearly right (one that is not obviously a loose fit at one end) can be tested by smearing it lightly with engineer's blue, trying it in the matching hole with a screwing motion and removing it again. The blue will be removed from the surface where the fit is tighter, showing how any adjustment should be made. If by chance (or sheer skill, of course) the taper is tight and difficult to remove, and the blue is rubbed off all the way along, well done.

The normal alternative method for taper turning is to offset the tailstock from its central position, moving the centre towards the operator, so that this method also produces a taper that narrows towards the tailstock. One way to do this is by moving the tailstock body in relation to its base; most lathes, except the very smallest, have a tailstock that can be adjusted in this way. What if you do not have an adjustable tailstock or it won't move far enough? Or you have spent some time getting the tailstock exactly central and you don't want to disturb it ever again? Either way, help is at hand. What you need is a device to mount in the tailstock taper that carries a separate centre that can be adjusted out of line. Two ways to do this are fairly ready to hand, relying on using a boring head or similar device fixed in the unmodified central tailstock, with a centre fitted in place of a boring tool. This presents an interesting work-holding problem. Whether you offset the tailstock or use an offset centre, problems can arise because conventional centres will not run exactly as they should in the work; quite simply, the two tapers of the centres themselves, male and female, do not fit properly together at either end of the offset work. For accurate work holding over an extended session, especially where the taper is more than a degree or so, this method of supporting the work can lead to disappointment, as the centres in the work fidget and are likely to become worn or distorted before the job is complete, reducing the accuracy just when you need it most. To help reduce this rubbing, you can use a special bell-type or trumpet-ended centre drill to produce the centre drillings in the work,

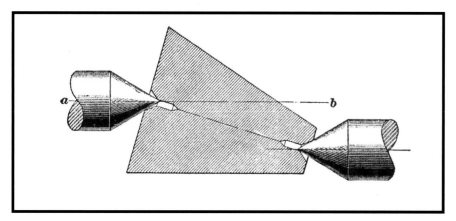

Fig. 4.3 The angle of taper here is exaggerated perhaps, but the problem is clear – the centres do not fit.

producing a flared hole rather than a true cone. This ensures that the fixed centre rubs around against a curved surface rather than the corner of a fixed 60-degree angle. Centres tipped with tungsten carbide are sometimes useful if wear proves to be a problem.

A further, more sophisticated, solution to this problem lies in the use of spherical, rather than pointed, male centres in the headstock and tailstock. The conical holes in the workpiece can remain the same as normal, although they do need to be a bit on the large size to work well, but their conical supports are replaced by hard steel ball-ends. This allows for the fidgeting or swivelling movement to take place over the surface of a part-sphere, with much less wear and tear of the rubbing surfaces. There are two main ways to make this change: firstly by using ball-ended centres in the mandrel and tailstock; or secondly by using hollow-ended centres (that is, with female cones at both ends) with off-the-shelf steel bearing balls between each pair of hollow centres. Both methods rely on special parts accurately made, which

seem not to be so readily available commercially, however. The first method requires either a pair of soft centres to be modified by removing the point by grinding or turning and milling or turning a ball end, followed by hardening and tempering, and then polishing the ball-end or alternatively, ball-ends to be made (and hardened and so on) on short pieces of round silver steel bar, held in collets at each end of the lathe. The new ball-ends locate in the work-

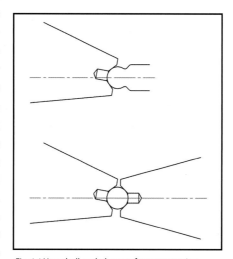

Fig. 4.4 Use a ball-ended centre for taper turning and, whatever the angle, rotation will not distort the rubbing surfaces.

piece centres already drilled.

For the second method, a pair of soft centres can again be the starting point with the ends turned or ground off. Each centre is held in the lathe mandrel in turn and the exposed end, now flat, is drilled with a centre drill to produce a conical hole about the same size as the holes in the workpiece. The work is then carried between these centres with a bearing ball in each end, fitted with a dab of grease every time, remembering to check the firmness of the tailstock in the work from time to time as turning progresses. Whichever method you use, the sizes of centres and balls should be chosen to ensure that the surfaces in contact are towards the outer edges of the 60-degree cones forming the female centres, but not resting only against the outer edges of the cones. Suitable loose balls are available in a wide range of sizes from commercial bearing and drive belt suppliers or your local bicycle shop.

At the headstock end, the ball centre can be held in a collet directly in the spindle taper, but it helps to fit the tailstock centre first. Use a boring head in the tailstock, set so that the adjustment moves the tools horizontally (that is, in the Y direction) and fit a ball-ended centre instead of a boring bar. The boring head must be drawn firmly into the mandrel taper with a drawbar (like the one used in the headstock but somewhat shorter) so that it cannot rotate, as this would ruin the job. Use a length of studding and a washer and nut perhaps, if you have no dedicated fitting. First though, fit the boring head briefly in the driven spindle and adjust the offset setting so that the ball turns

Fig. 4.5 Holding the ball-end in a boring head simplifies adjustment of the taper angle setting.

exactly centrally, and note the reading on the scale. When you take this reading, ensure that the inevitable backlash in the adjustment is taken up in the positive direction (in which the reading of the setting increases); this should ensure that as the required offset is adjusted, the dimension can be read off directly without worrying about the backlash or counting negative distances. This should ensure that the resulting taper should be fairly accurate, knowing the length between the middles of each of the two ball-end centres and the

required taper per foot. If you need to create a taper measured in degrees and minutes, rather than inches per foot in the old style, the calculation of the offset relies on the tangent of the angle, in relation to the between-ball-centres length. However you do the working out, it is likely that in practice you will not produce an accurate taper the first time, just as it requires skill and experience to make an accurate cylinder. Have a mating part ready as you get near to size and try it for fit. If it does wobble a bit on the work (quite likely) then look

closely at the gap around the end you can see. Just release the tailstock and slide it away down the bed, and if the large end of the taper at the headstock end shows a gap then the offset needs to be increased; if the gap is at the tailstock end, reduce it. The further movement required is about half the width of the gap, this indicates by how much to adjust the offset. Final fitting can be done using engineer's blue as detailed earlier.

If you don't have a boring head in your tool chest, a further alternative is to make up something that works in the same way as a boring head, but made especially for this offsetting when taper turning. There are tools, drawings and at least one kit of parts available to help you with this. The Projects section has more details, including the generating process for making ball-ended centres.

FIXED AND TRAVELLING STEADIES

There are times when you need to turn a fairly long bar that is too long to permit you to rely on holding it at one end only, but where it is not possible to use a centre to hold the outer end of the work. Perhaps the end is threaded, or damaged, or already has a hole that is too big or not accurately central, or you need to put a centre countersink in the end of a long length of plain round bar to start a series of machining operations. This is where a 'steady' can be helpful. Instead of locating in the end of your bar, these have adjustable arms that slide against a cylindrical section of the bar towards the outer end. The steady can be fixed to the bed of the lathe or to the tool carrier, moving along with it – but of course the latter method does require the workpiece to be cylindrical over the whole length where the steady will run.

If the workpiece is fairly flexible, it is too easy to set up the steady arms offset, so that the tailstock centre does not line up exactly with the centre around which the work is turning. The answer is to set up carefully in stages, first adjusting the work to rotate centrally (that is, not wobbling around as it rotates) and then adjusting the steady arms to rest

Fig. 4.6 *The fixed steady on the left clamps to the bed of the lathe to hold the outer end of a bar; the travelling steady moves with the tool holder to resist any distortion of the bar from cutting forces.*

Turning Between Centres • 33

against the work without pushing it to one side. What if the end of the bar is not round? In this case, a solution could be found by using (or making up) an extra tubular piece (called a 'barrel chuck') with four socket screws pointing inwards at each end to clamp around the work, carefully centred by adjusting its clamping screws, so that a cylindrical surface is provided for the steady. The exact details of the centring adjustment will depend on how any lumps and bumps are positioned, but a little ingenuity can go a long way in such matters. It is even possible, sometimes, to clamp the barrel chuck tube in place as accurately as can be managed and then to turn it in position using very light cuts to produce an accurate cylindrical surface for the steady arms. A travelling steady, which is fixed to the toolpost instead of to the lathe bed, can also be used to support a long thin workpiece when turning between centres, to help prevent any tendency for the work to bend or whip under pressure from the tool. In all cases the steady arms, which are usually bronze, must be carefully adjusted and well lubricated before starting the machining and checked from time to time for any temperature rise from friction, readjusting if necessary. The bronze arms will naturally tend to leave a witness where they have rubbed on the work, this can usually be removed by the use of fine emery cloth; if this surface is critical to the design, it might be better to arrange for a slightly oversize surface to be left on the work until after the steady has been used, and then turn (or grind) to a more precise, or a more appealing, finish.

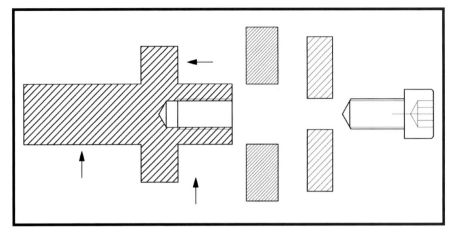

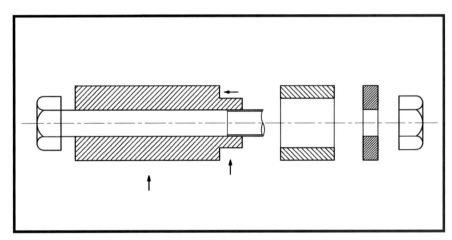

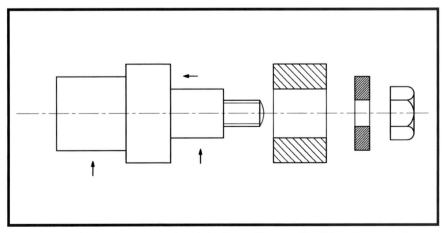

Fig. 4.7, Fig. 4.8 and Fig 4.9 Three versions of mandrel tools turned from round bar. If the surfaces arrowed are made without moving the mandrel in the chuck, concentricity should be preserved and good results obtained.

Fig. 4.10 A Morse Taper drill-chuck adapter can be used to carry a circular part pressed onto the outer taper using a bench vice.

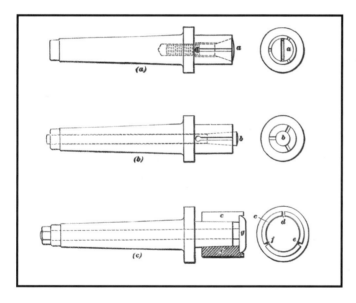

Fig. 4.11 Three styles of expanding mandrel made from soft-end Morse Taper fittings.

MANDRELS AND ARBORS

There are many turning jobs that cannot be held readily in a scroll chuck or collet, or between centres, and which need a more specialist fixture. Anything with a central hole that cannot be held in a chuck, perhaps because it is thin, or needs to be turned on both sides or edges at the same setting for true concentricity, can be held on a mandrel (sometimes also called an arbor). A mandrel can be made to size for a particular job and kept for further work of the same inside diameter or used for a smaller size by turning down the locating surface. All that is needed is a method to hold the mandrel concentric, for this purpose a collet is ideal. The sketches show the sort of thing that can be produced fairly easily, even if you are still part way up the learning curve with your lathe, starting with a length of round bright steel bar. If you are in a hurry for a simple job, perhaps reducing the outer diameter of a washer while leaving a good finish, a mandrel can be made with a slight taper on the holding diameter with the workpiece located on it with endwise pressure (from a tube in a bench vice, for example).

Another method starts with an MT taper fitting with a soft outer end, which can be machined in various ways to hold parts firmly. For a more adaptable solution, one that can be used for a range of sizes, you could make use of a set of expanding mandrels. These have a steel tube, cylindrical to hold in a chuck or collet, or with a Morse Taper at one end that can be held directly in the lathe, with a slow taper towards the other end where there is an accurate centre for the tailstock. The kit comes with a range of slotted sleeves of different outer diameters to slide over the taper. Each sleeve is matched inside to the angle of the taper and is ground truly cylindrical on the outside with a shoulder at one end. The workpiece is held on the cylinder and against the shoulder, and the sleeve is forced towards the large end of the taper, expanding it and holding the work in place. The tightening action relies on a thread inside the taper or in a knurled outer ring. The range of sizes covered by each sleeve is small, usually no more than one millimetre, so each complete kit will only cover a fairly small range of hole sizes. As the work is gripped only on its inner diameter, and it is not clamped firmly endways, turning operations using expanding

Fig. 4.12 This set of mandrels comprises a tapered inner bar onto which any of the range of sleeves can be carried to hold work by a central bore. ARC EURO TRADE LTD

mandrels should involve only sharp tools and light cuts, especially for thin parts such as washers. One difficulty you might find with a set of expanding mandrels is that they rely on the lathe and chuck being in excellent condition, especially regarding concentricity. If you have doubts about this, and this sort of accuracy is vital to the work in hand, a mandrel made specially for the job, and used without removing it from the chuck (and so disturbing its concentricity), is the answer. The Project section of this volume includes ideas for special mandrels that can be made without needing access to hardening or grinding equipment.

5 Workholding on the Vertical Mill

Holding work for milling usually involves clamping it directly to the table of the machine or to an additional fixture, such as a vice, a 'rotary table', an 'angle plate' or a combination of these. In most cases the same principles apply and reliance is often placed on T-nuts, studs and clamps.

The T-nuts fit into the slots in the table of the mill, rotary table or other attachment. Studs are screwed into the T-nuts and clamping bars, usually slotted, are held on the studs by washers and nuts. If the clamp is straight, the outer end is supported on a block of metal so the clamp is level and bears on the top face of the work. It can be

very helpful, if you are likely to need to remove the workpiece and return it for further work to the table or if a repetitive job is in progress, to use an extra washer and nut to hold the studs firmly in place before adding the clamps and tightening them. Of course, the nut and washer should be added to the bottom end of the stud before it is screwed into the T-nut. Although this clamping operation may seem straightforward, there are details that it is important to get right. The T-nuts should fit properly in the slots; if they are too small there is a risk that they will not bear properly on both sides at the top of the slot, this may cause breakage of the slot edges.

Cast iron is never very strong in tension. T-nuts that are too close a fit, however, will not slide easily into position and the risk is that the stud may be pulled over sideways, putting a concentrated load on the slot edges, again risking failure. If you have a clamping kit made for your model of mill, the sizes should be correct and this will give you a pattern for making additional T-nuts. Ideally, any extra table will have slots of the same size, but this is not always possible. If, for example, you have an old Myford lathe, but add to it a new mill, neither the slots nor the studs will be the same sizes. With a set for one machine though, you can make T-nuts for the other, following the guidance in these pages. In principle, it is better to keep inch-sized fittings for inch machines, but the wide availability of metric nuts and screws, along with the much higher prices asked for BSF threads to match a Myford, make such principles more difficult to apply. Whether you buy a set of T-nuts or make your own, it is important that there are no burrs or sharp edges, which would prevent the nuts from sliding to the correct positions in the slots. It is also important to ensure that the studs do not tighten through the nuts and against the bottom of the slot. If this happens, you can have a clamp that seems to be tight, but which is trapped in posi-

Fig. 5.1 A clamping stud fixed in place on the mill table using a washer and nut.

Fig. 5.2 *With the T-nut held inverted in a bench vice, a blunt chisel damages the thread to prevent studs from tightening down into the slot.*

you to choose a block that extends rather higher than the work, so that you can engage the end of the bar in the block teeth in order that the bar is more or less level. The raising blocks are in pairs in a range of sizes, any of which will fit together, and this gives an alternative method to achieve the height you need, with the flat base of the bar resting on the top of an inverted block. As always, things are not quite as simple as they seem.

First, the quality of finish of the parts in the kit may not be wonderful, perhaps with burrs or roughness on the clamping bars or the raising blocks, this may cause problems with looseness or marks on the work. It takes only a few minutes to tidy up the whole set, using a fine file and a sheet of emery.

Second, when the clamps are in line with the table slots, the raising blocks tend to be positioned directly over the slots in the table, bearing only on the slot edges, which are undercut and so not too strong. Either the bars should be rotated a few degrees on the studs, moving the block onto solid metal, or an extra plate of steel or light alloy should be used to spread the load on the table.

Third, it is important to look closely at the contact between the clamp and the work. Ideally, the clamp should be exactly level, spreading the load on the surface, and never tilted so that it bears only on the very edge of the work. This can be difficult and fiddly to achieve in practice, but there is an alternative that relies on making a simple extra part. All that is needed is a short length of steel or light alloy round bar sawn in half lengthwise and rubbed flat, or

tion and jacked up against the top of the slot by the stud, so do look out for this fault. Many T-nuts have the lowest thread bruised deliberately to prevent a stud passing right through; if yours are not made safe in this way, hold the nuts upside down in a bench vice and use a blunt cold chisel or centre punch to close up the last turn of thread in a couple of places. Do not be tempted to use ordinary hexagon-headed bolts or

coach bolts in place of T-nuts and studs. The bearing surface against the slot edges is too small for this sort of load, you risk serious damage.

The clamp bars supplied in a modern shop-bought kit are slotted for most of the length, with one end chamfered on the sides and top, and usually the other end is machined to an angled zigzag. These teeth match with teeth on raising blocks in the kit. This helps

Fig. 5.3 The zigzag faces of both angle-block and clamp bar provide a wide range of height settings.

Fig. 5.5 Curved surfaces from everyday odds and ends can be used for clamping jobs.

Fig. 5.4 Should the clamp bar not be exactly horizontal, the curved spacer and the radiused deep nut and washer will compensate.

perhaps for bigger work a short length of steel handrail section with a radius one side but flat on the other. This is placed with the flat side to the work and the clamp bearing on the curved side, it makes sure that even if the clamp is too high, or rather low, at the other end, the load is spread evenly over the job and not concentrated on one edge. Another sophistication that can help to make clamping really secure is the use of slightly domed nuts and hollowed washers in place of the flat-faced shouldered nuts provided with the kit. To work properly, any clamp nut needs to bear on the clamp all the way round. This is clearly not possible with a slotted clamp, so a plain washer can be used to spread the load a bit more effectively. But it all still relies on the clamp being exactly horizontal, at right angles to the vertical stud, and this is rarely possible. In the Projects section you will find details of how to make up more effective nuts and washers with part-spherical bearing faces, and without needing fancy material or elaborate tooling. Another possibility can help when the work, or the working parts of the machine, get in the way of

Fig. 5.6 Short faceplate clamps from Myford can be of use to us all, and for milling too.

Fig. 5.7 The stud to the right pulls the clamp down, against resistance from the left one – a very useful resource if space is tight.

a conventional clamping arrangement, or there is simply no room for the necessary stud. The solution might lie in an elaboration of the clamping idea, where a bridge of metal from the work to a raising block or another component is held downwards not by a stud directly, but by a further clamp relying on a stud further away. Here again we come across the problem that two surfaces transmitting forces are not likely to be exactly flat against each other. A solution to this for the bridge piece is to rely on a conventional clamping bar, with the extra clamp resting on a part-spherical surface rather than a flat one. For this you need a 'coach bolt' with a square on the shank, small enough to fit in your clamp slots. An ordinary M10 coach bolt should fit in the slots of an M10 clamping kit just right. The thread and the length do not matter at all – in fact it is better to cut off the threaded part but leave the square in place with the domed head. Drop this into the slot in your clamp and rest the second clamp onto the radiused surface. Save the threaded offcuts for when you need very short studs, perhaps when fly-cutting, for example.

Where the space needed for a relatively long clamping bar is simply not available, an alternative might be found using the short clamps originally produced for Myford Lathes as faceplate clamps. These have a short slot and a flat tab at one end that locates on the workpiece. Two T-nuts are added to the same table slot, each is fitted with a stud. Each stud carries a nut and washer, followed by the faceplate clamp, a further washer and nut on the nearer of the two studs, which holds the clamp down, and the outer stud nut below the clamp can then be adjusted to ensure that the clamp is level and firm before tightening the clamping stud. It may not be clear from this description that the outer stud (away from the workpiece) is under a compression load, so in this case the T-nut is bearing on the base of the slot and the load is produced by pushing the outer

Fig. 5.8 A stud held firmly down onto the table provides support for a short clamp as a locating stop for the workpiece.

end of the clamp upwards. This assembly works well with M10, or ⅜in studs, as the slots in the Myford parts are made with a sensible clearance. With smaller studs it may be that thick, large diameter washers are also needed, and for M12 studs the slots may need to be eased by filing to make enough room or you might find it easier to use the same principle with the shortest slotted clamp in an M12 kit.

The advice about forces from the cutting tool apply here, so check in particular that your clamping arrangement is strong in the right directions. A further safeguard against movement could be an additional stud in a T-nut, with a small slotted clamp adjusted to locate against the work, or a slab of steel, drilled through and bolted firmly to the table in contact with the workpiece to hold it against sideways movement. In the Projects section you will find further ideas to ensure that the clamp loads are always applied centrally where they are needed, not on the outer corners, as well as a method of fixing a stop to the vice itself.

Most milling machines, made for use in the shed rather than the factory, have a fairly narrow bed with three T-slots running its length. This tends to limit your options when clamping work, as the slots are not always in the most useful positions. A solution to this is very easily made up using simple processes – see the Projects section for full details of a suggested bridge piece.

HOLDING WORK FOR MILLING IN A MACHINE VICE

A wide range of vices are available for this role, but one thing must be clear from the start – a drill vice is not good enough. We need a vice that is solidly made, with a moving jaw that remains always parallel to the fixed one, accurately at right angles to the base, properly flat all over and machined so that the flat area below the jaws, where many of the workpieces will locate, is truly parallel to the base and to the tops of the jaws. It also needs a method to fix the vice firmly to the machine table and, if possible, to turn the jaws through a set angle and lock them in position. You might find the right tool listed as a machine vice, precision vice, milling vice or toolmaker's vice, whereas the drill vice tends to be fairly light and thin, what you need is going to look solid and heavy. Indeed, it will be heavy – lifting a full-sized industrial version is certainly a two-handed job for ordinary mortals. Of course, the price goes up with size as well as quality, and when you are starting out there is a temptation to look for the cheapest, but remember that while a big vice can hold small parts, a small one is useless for anything big. But you've only got a small machine? Here it can be the height of the vice that is the limitation, so look for a vice that is relatively shallow and do not be tempted at this stage by fancy tilting features, which

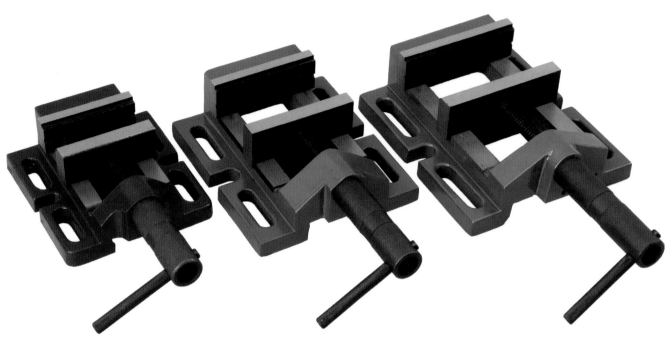

Fig. 5.9 ARC: Premium Engineers Drill Vices. Ideal for use on a pillar drill, but not for milling operations. ARC EURO TRADE LTD

further use up lots of space. A swivel base is still very handy though, as this enables you in many awkward cases to turn the vice so that the cut is towards the fixed jaw, as recommended.

A handy tool, detailed in the Projects section, can be used to align a machine vice accurately with the worktable, if you find any difficulties using an engineer's square for this task. A rectangle of steel is machined accurately so that the sides are at right angles and a flat bar to fit the T-slots is bolted firmly to it, also at right angles. Checks are made to ensure that the bar is exactly square to the sides of the plate and soft solder, or Loctite, can then be used to make the joint between them permanent. Ideally such a square would be made from 'gauge plate', properly hardened, tempered and ground to size, but for all ordinary purposes a mild steel plate will be a good start. Just don't drop it

on a concrete floor. In use, the square tool rests with the narrow bar in the T-slot and it is slid against the machined vice edge before it is tightened down, locating it accurately so that the jaws are in line with the table movement. If your vice is not supplied with its edges

machined to assist in this process, the procedure is to obtain a bar of steel that fits accurately in your T-slots. Bright mild steel is ideal, or use a length of square 'key steel', as the surface as supplied should be smooth and quite flat enough for our purposes; about 200mm

Fig. 5.10 A chunky machine vice that will meet the need of accuracy and strength. AXMINSTER TOOL CENTRE LTD

Fig. 5.11 This simple home-made tool can speed up the job of squaring a vice to the bed. The crossbar locates into a bed slot and the side fits against the vice edge.

is a sensible length, but do check that the bar is good and straight. Clamp the bar horizontally in the vice so that some width of the bar projects above the jaws (perhaps half the width if you have a square bar, for example) and turn the vice over so that the bar slides into a table slot, locating the vice in position but upside down. Use packing to ensure that the base of the vice is parallel to the table, clamp it all firmly in place. Now you can skim the two edges of the vice base with a milling cutter, cleaning up the edges of the casting to provide useful flat locating faces each side. As the unmachined surface of the vice casting is likely to be hard, and to include sand particles, a cutter made of tungsten carbide is to be preferred for this work. An HSS cutter will serve, but in this case do not use a brand new tool as the edges are likely to lose some of their keenness in the process. All that is needed is a bright machined surface on both sides of the base so that each will locate against the square; anything wider than the thickness of your square

should be plenty in most cases. If the shape of the vice does not allow for this sort of treatment, it is possible to machine a shallow groove across the base of the vice (again held upside down on the worktable and located in the T-slot), the same width as your T-slots, and fix in place a strip of bright mild steel the same width but thicker than the groove; perhaps for this another length of square 'key steel' would serve

Fig. 5.12 Some vices are supplied as cast around the base, so a machining operation is needed to provide a locating face square to the jaws.

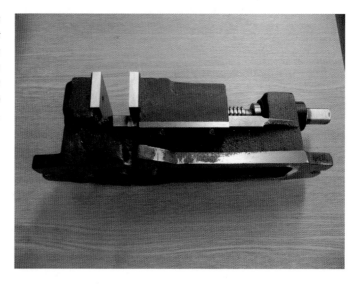

nicely. The strip can be held in place using an engineering adhesive or by adding two countersunk screws near the ends, or perhaps using both of these methods. When the vice is turned back over, the strip will be used to locate in a T-slot, so be sure to position the groove and the locating bar so that they do not interfere with the positions of the slots for hold-down bolts or studs. Here is an alternative method to arrange this ready-to-use vice aligning method in cases when the bar and the holding slots would otherwise coincide. The locating strip has a tab riveted to each end, the tabs are screwed to the base of the vice assembly.

The methods just described will not always produce toolroom precision, so if you are in any doubt about the accuracy of your vice, or your fitting arrangements, or if you are using borrowed equipment or are short of time, there is another way to ensure that the jaws are accurately aligned with the movement of the table. This relies on the use of sacrificial spacing blocks, which can be of

Fig. 5.13 Where no flat surface is available, a slot bar can be fixed like this one.

Fig. 5.14 Alternative light alloy jaws are fitted to a vice and the locating slot is machined in situ, resulting in perfect alignment with the bed.

bright mild steel or light alloy, between the vice jaws. Whatever you use, choose blocks that are known to be properly flat and undamaged on one face at least, and use those faces outwards, against the vice jaws. The blocks need to be at least as long as the jaws, and at least as tall as the space between them, and about 10mm thick. If possible, apply a thin smear of rubber adhesive to the known flat faces of each block and allow the solvent a few minutes to evaporate, before tightening the vice as normal with the blocks in place and leaving it overnight. This sticking process will ensure that the blocks remain in position in use, but that they are not so firmly fixed as to make removal difficult. You can use Loctite in a similar way and rely on heat to soften it later. A domestic oven at 200°C should work well, but do be careful as the vice will remain hot for some time. Of course, you could set up new jaws with the standard vice jaws removed and new softer light alloy alternatives of around the same thickness bolted in place using the same fasteners; this saves messing about with adhesive and is a good way to make the best of an old worn vice or one with damaged jaws.

To produce the accurate vice slot you need, clamp down the vice in about the correct position, open the jaws rather wider than the part to be machined, insert another block of metal about as wide as the component to be machined and known to have parallel sides, clamping it about centrally between the new spacing blocks, raising it on packing if necessary. Tighten the vice firmly so that the packing piece is held securely between

Fig. 5.15 A workpiece sits firmly in the newly machined corners for the next operation.

the new spacer blocks. Then use an end mill or slotting cutter to machine a notch (about 5mm deep and 2mm wide, say) in the inner edges of each of the new spacers in turn. Take finishing cuts that remove a small amount of metal from both faces of each notch, so that the result is square right into the corners and use exactly the same height setting both sides so that the slots match perfectly. This ensures that the notch that will be used to carry the workpiece is exactly aligned with the movement of the table, both horizontally and vertically, even if the fitting of the vice or the movement of the table is somewhat cockeyed.

Before you release the pressure on the vice to remove the packing pieces, do remember to remove the burrs that arise from the machining operation, perhaps by running a smooth flat file at

45 degrees across both cut edges and across their ends on both sides. Until you remove the holding nuts for the

vice, the newly cut notch can be used with confidence in its alignment with the X movement of the mill, so do think before you start this process to choose the spacing blocks and notch size that will serve all your current needs for this sort of milling work. Once the vice holding down nuts are loosened, the alignment is lost, but as long as you leave the spacing blocks stuck (or bolted) in place and pack the jaws to the width needed for a new job, proper alignment can be restored by bolting the vice back in its approximate position (or even on a different machine) and remachining the notches both sides as before, removing as little metal as is needed to clean up the surfaces.

Clamping a plain vice to the worktable is not the only way to proceed. When a machined surface is needed at an angle other than 90 degrees to the table, you can use a tilting vice or fix a standard vice to a tilting table.

Fig. 5.16 ARC: 130-040-00400 Tilting Vice. A tilting vice allows for accurate angular cuts to be made without complex setting up. ARC EURO TRADE LTD

Fig. 5.17 A steel plate fixed to a round bar makes up the major part of this home-made angle vice.

This home-made fixture used for fairly shallow angles is detailed in the Projects section. It comprises a flat slab of mild steel fixed to a round bar. The bar is held in shallow V-blocks located by the table T-slots (for squareness) and the free edge of the slab is held up by an adjustable screw and dome nut. A machining vice can be bolted across the flat surface, or along it, or at any angle. A tool like this can simplify the manufacture of parts where the edges need to be machined properly flat, but not at right angles. An alternative method is to rely on the milling head tilting to one side and moving the table

and the workpiece in the Y direction. This is a perfectly sensible way to cut metal, but this limits the travel and therefore

Fig. 5.18 Locating blocks for the home-made angle vice fit over blocks in T-slots, while the round bar rests in the shallow V.

the length that can be machined at one pass, to about the width of the table. If a fairly long part (such as a 'gib strip') needs to be machined at an angle along the whole length, it can be difficult to hold it securely in a vice because of distortion of the overhanging parts. In this case, it can be helpful to attach the workpiece to a long piece of steel that is much thicker and to clamp the steel rigidly at both ends as well as centrally. An adhesive can be helpful for this (if the machining is going to be gentle, with shallow cuts, shellac would be adequate). If necessary, start with an extra length of stock and mill a short flat at each end of the steel at the appropriate angle, use these flats to clamp the ends securely onto 'raising blocks' on the table, or drill and countersink holes in the extra length for small screws. The workpiece can then be clamped to the central section of the steel using three or four 'toolmaker's clamps', moving them in stages along the work as machining proceeds, so that the work is always held firm.

THE ROTARY TABLE AND THE DIVIDING HEAD

Some work on a milling machine requires you to turn the workpiece around an axis, either from one position to another, perhaps to drill a circle of holes, or continuously so that a curved surface can be produced, such as the radius around the end of a bar. A rotary table will serve well for most of these jobs; only when you need to divide the rotation into an even wider range of different steps, or at an angle, does a dividing head come into its own.

Rotary tables comprise, in essence, a flat surface to mount on the mill table on which is carried in bearings a circular plate with slots to allow work to be held in the same manner as with a

Fig. 5.19 One complete turn of the handle turns a worm gear and rotates the head by 9 degrees. A set of plates with a wide range of drillings allows the head to be rotated by exact fractions of a turn and fractions of a degree.

Fig. 5.20 Similar in the main workings to a dividing head, the rotary table lacks a tilting option and so is cheaper and lower than its bigger brother. AXMINSTER TOOL CENTRE LTD

lathe faceplate, or to mount a chuck or collet holder. The circular plate has gear teeth cut around its lower edge (inside and not visible), engaging with a worm alongside that can be turned by a handle and the outer visible edge of the plate has a scale in degrees. A smaller scale rotating with the handle allows parts of a turn to be measured, in the same way as the calibrated scales work on lathe and mill controls, and on traditional micrometers. Knowing the number of teeth around the plate, it is a simple matter to know how many turns and how many divisions are needed to turn through any angle. The normal design has ninety teeth on the gear so that one complete turn of the handle moves the surface through 4 degrees and the dial markings on the handle are at one-minute spacings. One edge

of the base has a flange allowing the device to be mounted with its axis horizontal, a dedicated tailstock can also be used, bolted to the mill table so that long workpieces can be held horizontally for slots, keyways and gear teeth to be milled at the required angular positions.

The range of sizes readily available (without straying into industrial sizes) is from 75mm diameter to 200mm; on the larger sizes the centre bore is machined to a Morse Taper to take an additional range of holding tools. The only other factor you need to consider when looking to add one to your kit is the design of chuck you already have. Rotary tables may have three or four T-slots for mounting chucks and you need to check that your chuck attachment is compatible, especially in the

smaller sizes and for use with a smaller mill where the height above the table is very limited. It is always possible to make up a separate mounting plate to hold an incompatible chuck, but this all takes time, makes setting up more complicated and uses up the available height. The final fitting, sometimes only available as an extra, is a dividing plate for the handle. This has a series of rings of holes, allowing the handle to be positioned accurately without peering at the scales for every small rotation, making it easier to set the table position to the desired angular positions. The dividing plate fits onto the body of the tool, behind the handle on the table, with a spring-loaded peg on the handle that engages in the selected hole and locates the handle precisely at the chosen position.

Even with a dividing plate in use, the rotary table does not allow the choice of angular positions available with a fully equipped dividing head. The mechanism here is very much the same, but with one further trick up its sleeve. The body is made in two parts, one able to turn within the other like a tilting vice. This allows the rotating head and chuck assembly to be positioned at any angle between horizontal and vertical, and entirely independent of the rotation of the head itself. This is very handy if you need a series of holes spaced exactly around in a circle but at an angle to the axis, such as the spoke holes in the hub for a wire wheel. It is handy too, for milling of any description at an angle, as long as the workpiece can be held in the chuck or a collet or on a faceplate in place of the chuck. The machine is supplied with (usually) four dividing plates, so the range of divisions and angles available is even more comprehensive. This makes it just what you need for making gear wheels in a range of sizes, as might be required for a model gearbox or a full-sized clock. One further problem a dividing head can help you to solve is to manage circular parts that are too big to fit above the bed of your lathe. Set the work at an angle on the dividing head, then set the mill head at a similar angle, the radius you can machine is limited by the length of your milling table. Machining all the way round your traction engine wheel in this way is going to take an hour or two, but the alternative is to seek out a machine shop with a spare big lathe and the time and inclination to help.

Are these dividing heads expensive? Yes, as you might expect. Other disadvantages? Well, they are fairly heavy as an assembly, so are not something to send through the postal system very often. And tall too, so only useful if you have a middle-sized milling machine or a proper full-sized industrial model. One final comment if you do decide that a dividing head is the answer to your prayers. The centre bore of many such devices is made not to a Morse Taper but to a Browne & Sharpe standard with a rather less steep taper. This means that finding a collet holder is not so easy and you may find, as I did, that the USA is the only source of such equipment. Similar concerns may also apply to the thread on which a chuck is carried.

6 Boring and Milling on the Lathe

In principle, there is little difference between a lathe and a mill. Normal lathe work has the job rotating quickly and a slowly moving cutting tool, whereas a mill has a rapidly rotating cutter and a slowly moving workpiece. If the work and the tool are interchanged, a lathe can be used for milling (and vice versa, but nowhere near so often in practice). Holding a milling cutter in a lathe is easy – and with a collet system in the headstock firmness and accuracy should be guaranteed. What is needed is a fitting to hold the work so that it can be moved in any of three directions, to and fro, in and out, and up and down; or in engineering terms, in the directions X, Y and Z. The answer is fairly simple. The job can be fixed in place of the tool holder of the lathe, using conventional work-holding methods, and moved along the bed or across it (X and Y) by the normal control handles while the cutter in the headstock does its work. Up and down (Z) movement requires extra fittings for milling operations, but most lathe manufacturers have made tooling available for everything except the smallest and cheapest machines.

Even if you cannot find the 'correct' kit for your model, it is usually possible to adapt something made for a machine of similar size to do the job. As the toolpost usually sits on the flat surface of the cross-slide with its T-slots, it is simple to remove the toolpost itself and replace it with a milling adaptor based on an angle plate with an extra, vertical, slide with its own feed screw. With a bit more sophistication, the angle plate can be located on a short central boss fitting in place of the toolpost stud, so it can be turned around the vertical axis and set at an angle; a further adaptor sometimes enables the extra feed to be moved away from the vertical. This enables the milling processes to cope with compound angles, which are not needed very often but very useful when they are. Remember though, that every slide has to have some clearance in its mounting to allow it to move and the more complex the set-up, the more slack there will be to interfere with the firmness that produces accuracy and avoids chatter. In consequence, you should take shallow cuts and proceed gently, checking as you go in case anything has shifted during the cutting processes. The work is clamped to the vertical table in the normal way, generally using T-nuts and clamps (*see* Chapter 5). All this may seem to make a milling machine unnecessary, and it is certainly true that some engineers have used their lathes to produce excellent work in this way. There are limitations though, on the rigidity you can achieve with fixtures bolted to a lathe cross-slide and on the size of component that can safely be held.

CYLINDER BORING

Another job that is a required task for model steam enthusiasts, among others, is boring a cylinder. The lathe can be set up for this using a boring bar. The work is clamped firmly to the standard lathe cross-slide, perhaps using a raising block, so that the axis of the cylinder coincides with the centre line of the headstock and tailstock. Alternatively, the work can be held on the vertical fitting used for milling in the lathe. This is a less firm mounting as there are more separate components connected together, but it allows for the height of the workpiece to be adjusted much more readily. The cutting tool, usually ground to the same shape as a turning tool, is carried in a hole running across a long and rigid bar, which itself is carried between centres at each end and driven by a dog attached to it at the headstock end. Boring is done by rotating the boring bar, slowly traversing the cylinder along the lathe bed so that the cutting tool moves steadily through the cylinder, cutting a cylindrical hole as it goes. Several passes are usually required, each taking out a small cut, until the whole of the inside surface shows even and regular machining marks. Since many cylinders, even at the casting stage, incorporate holes and slots to let the steam, or the fuel mixture in and out, the finishing operations need to be done with special care if the interrupted cuts are to produce accurate surfaces without chatter marks.

The task that will engage your workholding skills is the accurate positioning of the casting – it usually is a casting, in brass or cast iron – so that it is as nearly concentric as you can make it and firm enough to resist an interrupted cut, which is likely at least at the start of the machining operation. For this important role, it may be best to make up a special mild-steel plate that can be located and fixed down using the T-slots in the toolpost mounting surface, with additional holes in the new plate exactly where they are needed to mount the casting. Before starting the cut, check that the tailstock is properly in line with the headstock and tighten down all the locking devices for the saddle and cross-slide travel, except of course, the one that locks the saddle endways. This should prevent any tendency for the slides and the work to shuffle about as the cut proceeds.

Of course, you don't have to bore your cylinder in this way. It may be that it would be better to mount the casting on a faceplate and bore with a tool held in the toolpost or the tailstock. Mounting and balancing the cylinder is more complicated this way, but adjusting the tool to the required size of the bore is much easier, as the next chapter will explain.

7 Turning on a Faceplate

Here the workpiece is fixed firmly to a faceplate on the lathe mandrel for turning or boring operations in place of the more conventional chuck. This method of working can be especially useful if you have no milling machine. In this case, you may have skipped the earlier discussion on the vertical mill (*see* Chapter 5), but you may find it helpful to read it through. Most of the work-holding methods and principles covered there are very relevant to fixing work on a faceplate. Just as you do for milling, you will need a stock of bolts, nuts and washers, and some clamps and spacers. Work out what is going to be useful and collect a boxful before you start. Old nuts, scrap ball bearing races, offcuts of thick-walled tube squared off in the lathe, all come in handy for this sort of job. Light-alloy offcuts used as spacers can help to reduce out-of-balance problems on a faceplate and can be easier to machine to an exact size when required. If you have T-nuts that fit the slots on the faceplate, use them, as you can then do the tightening all from the one side. Watch out, though, for T-nuts that are crimped at the end of the thread. This detail is intended to stop a stud passing through the nut when holding down to a T-slot; unfortunately it stops these T-nuts being so useful with a faceplate, unless you are careful to choose studs as short as pos-

sible. My preference for this bolting down job is to use home-made T-nuts to suit the faceplate slots; and hexagon socket cap screws (commonly called Allen screws) as they are easy to fit and tighten and are always made of good strong steel. Accumulate a selection of these, of a range of lengths but all the same thread (to match your T-nuts) and you will only need the one key or spanner to fix them. Attachment can be by bolting directly through the job where suitable holes exist, or by the use of metal clamps or straps, either off-the-shelf or custom made. Do take particular care to use fastenings that are no longer than they need be. The whole faceplate assembly will be whirling round and there should be no chance of anything catching on the lathe, the toolpost, or on you the operator or your clothing, as work proceeds.

The workpiece may be located directly against the flat face of the faceplate, if a relevant flat surface exists for this on the workpiece, or it can be held away from the faceplate by spacers. You might need to turn down spacers to get the heights correct: just refit your three-jaw chuck to do this, while the faceplate remains horizontal on the bench. If the turning job on the workpiece involves an interrupted cut, quite likely in these cases, there will be a tendency to nudge the workpiece

every rotation, moving the work slowly but surely out of true and quite likely spoiling it. To help avoid this, add locating stops: short thick tubes can be fixed with bolts through the faceplate where they can locate the work securely against the forces generated by the cutting tool. Considerable ingenuity may be required to ensure that the work is properly located. Even when this is achieved a further problem remains, that of balance. Extra fittings, change gears or bits of scrap should be attached to correct this, and good balance is established by disconnecting the lathe spindle drive to allow the faceplate to turn naturally so that the heavy part is lowest. Then add material to the lighter side (at the top) and try again. It might be necessary to add weight where there is an existing holding bolt: try replacing the bolt with a longer one, with the extra weight made up by washers or nuts, or an example from your set of change gears.

Continue until the spindle, when turned by hand and released, has no tendency to stop in any particular orientation. If this cannot be done, perhaps because the drive cannot be disconnected readily or the spindle does not turn freely, proceed with caution. If this balancing is going to be a regular task, a dummy headstock spindle could be made up, turning on

Fig. 7.1 Any object of the right weight will serve as a balance; change gears are handy and come in a range of sizes.

ball bearings, to speed up the balancing process. Making a fixture for this is covered as a Project. Without a properly balanced job, engage the lowest speed and operate the clutch slowly, so that if vibration becomes serious you can stop the rotation before it gets out of hand. Turning very slowly takes longer, but it may be that this is still quicker than taking hours to achieve good balance before you start to cut metal. If the cut is intermittent, metal will be removed

from one side only, so the balance is going to change as work proceeds. Do remember though, that if the lathe is vibrating, this will affect the position of the tooling and accentuate any slack in the system, so accuracy and finish may suffer.

In practice it may be helpful to remove the faceplate and carry out the bolting operation with it flat on the bench, as this should simplify the positioning of any clamps or spacers.

Without gravity working against you, it is easier to hold everything steady at the same time. Once you are confident you have mastered the problem, tighten everything up firmly and test every part to be sure it is securely clamped and cannot move. Then fix the faceplate to the lathe and make final adjustments by slackening off the relevant nuts – not too much – and centralize the work by knocking it into position with a plastic-faced mallet, finally tightening

Fig. 7.2 These four simple additions to a faceplate can speed up the centring process.

the clamps. If concentricity is vital, check with a dial gauge as you turn the spindle by hand. In this case, it may be helpful to make up locating blocks with a screw adjustment to clamp in the faceplate slots, rather than relying on a gentle tap or two. Details may be found later in the Project. Don't forget that a central draw-bolt passing through the lathe mandrel can sometimes be used to pull the work firmly against the faceplate (when the faceplate is fitted to the lathe), if you cannot make

room for a full set of clamps. Studding is the ideal material for this. Then try to establish the balance before a slow test run.

If you need to carry out machining on work carried on the faceplate and then to remove the part and replace it after more machining or checking, make sure that the work is fully located by fixed parts that remain in place when the work clamps are removed. This means you should only need to set up and centralize once, but do check before

you cut, every time. To avoid having too many fixings, or running out of holes or slots to use, try to make fixings serve a dual role. Use a stud that is rather longer than you need when adding a locating fixture, and tighten the securing nut. Then use the rest of the thread to hold a clamp securing the work. This allows you to loosen the clamp to remove the work without disturbing the location, all on the same length of thread. If you can use this double-fixing method for all your clamps on a faceplate, it will simplify adjustments as there is less chance of slackening a nut only to find the whole fixing sliding away from its carefully measured position.

One difficulty with work on a faceplate is the positioning of parts, by which I mean sliding them sideways from an approximate position to an accurate one. This is because the slots are normally arranged like the petals of a daisy, so that they are all at 45-degree angles. Moving a part across the faceplate requires all its attachments to move in the same directions, this is not possible. One solution comprises a new faceplate with slots running parallel, with an angle plate that can therefore slide sideways for adjustment. A kit is available to make your own from castings; details are given in the Projects section.

8   Other Workholding Methods

USING OTHER WORKSHOP MACHINES

There are many different machines to be found in hobby workshops, often of a more specialized nature. Some, such as engraving machines, shapers, planers, slotting machines, drill presses and horizontal mills, are very similar in their requirements for work holding to those already discussed. Others, such as tool grinders and surface grinders, are better dealt with under the heading of Tool and Cutter Sharpening, while those such as band saws, polishing machines and finishers rely almost universally on hand-held operations. A collection of pliers can be very handy when your fingers might get too close to moving

parts for comfort, and when handwork rather than machining is required. There are a few holding methods though, that can help with particular problems, rather than applying to particular machines or processes, and they are included below.

HOLDING THIN FLAT PARTS

It is sometimes difficult to hold thin parts in cases, such as the sides of a model locomotive frame, where the mill is used as a small jig-borer for marking hole positions, and the whole of the surface needs to be accessible. Anything like a conventional clamp or clip simply gets in the way. One answer is to use adhesive, fixing the part to a

thicker or wider base layer, which can be clamped down well away from the work surface. This base plate might be steel, light alloy, MDF or even plywood, and located against stops fitted to the table so that it can be removed and replaced in exactly the same position. In the days before modern plastics, shellac varnish was used to hold the work down on the backing; the shellac was dissolved in alcohol, usually ethanol, and painted onto the surfaces in a thin layer. Removal involved heat and traces of the shellac were removed using alcohol again. Alternatively, a thin layer of shellac varnish would be applied to a backing piece and the warmed-up workpiece pressed down onto it and held until the shellac had hardened. It worked, indeed it is still used, but the shellac is very sensitive to changes in temperature. Get it too hot and it softens, too cold and it becomes brittle.

These problems have been overcome to a great extent by modern science and better results can now be achieved using thread-lock or PVA-based adhesives. Heating the work to separate it after machining operations can be done with a hairdryer or hot-air gun (the sort of thing used to apply heat-shrink tubing) or by immersion in really hot water. The difficulty you need to face is that these adhesives are

Fig. 8.1 A range of pliers is needed to hold work for filing, polishing or manipulating.

Fig. 8.2 *Ideal for holding small twist drills when drilling sheet metal, pin vices are also handy when working with wire.*

not really designed for such temporary jobs and removing traces from the workpiece may prove time-consuming. There are many solvents to try, but start with acetone, always remembering that many of these products are very flammable and the fumes are likely to irritate, so do this work outside and in a breeze, if you can. Before you get to work on a real workpiece, do not ignore the value of experimenting with the old-established method with shellac, perhaps using painter's knotting (which is shellac in alcohol and more readily available than raw shellac) as a varnish on the work, which is then laid in place while the surface is still sticky. Practise with any new or untried adhesive material in the same way, until you are familiar with its quirks.

Further problems arise when making flat parts from very thin sheet metal, such as shim washers. Steel shims in particular, which are tough to cut, need to be held firmly while this is done. Fortunately, many shims require a hole in the centre, but often the

outer edge has extra smaller holes and a wavy edge to fit around the mating parts. The method I have found most helpful in awkward cases is to trap a piece of shim, coated on both sides with knotting, between two pieces of plywood or MDF with parallel edges, one of which is marked on the face with an accurate tracing of the required shape. This assembly is held together by a ring of small bolts around the outside. Then position the centre of the inner hole on a drill press or mill table (where the parallel edges are handy) and use a hole-saw to cut out the central hole as near to the finished size as you can. Go slowly and use cutting oil for the steel, and avoid getting it too hot as the shellac will melt. Clamp the assembly edgeways (with the hole axis horizontal) in a bench vice and use a smooth half-round file to enlarge the hole to fit the component over which it will be used. Now you need two extra washers of steel or light alloy, big enough to overlap the inner hole edges, and use a central bolt to clamp

the whole assembly firmly together. This allows you to remove the outer bolts and to start work on removing material from the outside edge. Start with a thin-blade angle grinder and then a file, holding the assembly edgeways again in the bench vice and following the tracing on the surface. Before removing the central bolt, set the assembly horizontally on the table of a mill and use a small centre drill to position each of the small hole centres carefully, followed by an end mill to cut out the holes to the full size before moving on to position the next one in turn. Finally the centre bolt can be released and the assembly dropped into hot water to soften the shellac. Any residue can then be removed with alcohol (methylated spirit, burning alcohol) and the shim tidied up with careful use of a bench grinder, if you are confident and have a steady hand, followed by a fine file. Just this once, you should wear gloves for these final operations to avoid cuts from the sharp edges.

If the shim you need is a simple one, in effect a very thin plain washer, the same processes can be used to trap a piece of knotting-coated shim between plywood surfaces. Then drill a central hole the size of the guide drill in your hole saw (usually ¼in). This time, use the hole saw to cut the outer edge first and stop cutting as soon as you have cut through the shim, leaving one side of the plywood in sound condition. Then turn the assembly over and cut the inner edge with the hole saw, again holding it by the outer surfaces of the plywood. Separate the parts and clean up in the same way, keeping the piece from the centre as it may serve as a smaller shim in future.

LESS CONVENTIONAL WORK-HOLDING METHODS

There are times when standard work-holding tools will not serve, perhaps when working on delicate finished parts, such as clock hands or tiny washers, or parts that are too long to go in your lathe (or in your shed, perhaps). Thinking outside the box can often provide solutions. The first thing to remember is that hands and fingers have been developed over millennia as holding devices. An engineer needing to remove burrs from a newly made part might think about looking for a bench vice to hold the part, and soft jaws to avoid marking the work. By the time he has found what he needs, however, he could have held the part in one hand and a smooth file in the other and finished all the edges perfectly.

And so should you. Just remember that until you have removed them, the burrs may be sharp and unless you work frequently with your fingers in this sort of work, your skin will be delicate and easily cut, so wrap the part in a rag while you file. It also helps to fix an offcut of wood in the vice, so that the part can rest against it while filing.

THE PIN VICE

When you need to hold a wire or a similar thin part for filing, or to drill a very small hole, a pin vice is the answer. There are many patterns, all basically a very small drill-type chuck on a tubular metal handle. With some, the tiny collets within the chuck are supplied in two or more hole sizes; with others you need to acquire a set of three or four to cover the range. The sleeve around the chuck can be knurled for good grip so that drills can be held firmly; others have six, or eight, flats, which are helpful

if you need to file a part to a square or hexagon. Most of them have a hole right through so that you can deal with long parts, such as bicycle spokes or point your own knitting needles; some are double ended, and with double-ended collets; others come with a cap or knob that swivels, enabling the tool to be held normal to the work with one hand, while the other does the twiddling to rotate a drill bit. You can even make your own fairly easily, if you need to, perhaps based on the split collets available for small rotary tools, such as the Dremel range. Sizes range from collets with sharp edges that close down to nothing, up to about 5mm on sizes used by jewellers and watchmakers. As well as holding thin parts for further work, the larger sizes of pin vice are very useful as handles for needle files, especially if you have a lot of intricate filing to do.

9   Tool Holding

Fig. 9.1 The standard square block tool holder supplied with many small lathes; the tool height is adjusted with shim strips.

The standard tool holder provided with a modern lathe is likely to be a square block of steel bolted to the tool platform, with a slot along each vertical face, and above each slot a row of small screws. The cutting tool fits into the slot and the screws hold it in place. The height of the top of the cutting edge of the tool in relation to the mandrel centre is critical, this is adjusted using steel strips below the tool to bring it to the correct height. The four slots allow for a selection of tools, all adjusted in this way, to be brought into position by rotating the tool block. Sometimes a ratchet is fitted within the block so that it can be located accurately as each tool is rotated into position. This involves nothing very complicated but may be rather time-consuming, as many jobs can require the use of more than four tools, and every time a tool is fitted the height check and adjustment is needed. This problem has exercised the minds of many over the years, several different designs are available that are intended to speed up the setting process and ensure that a tool can be removed and later replaced in exactly the same position.

The term Quick Change Tool Post (QCTP) sounds like a standard sort of fitment, like a Morse Taper or a Metric Thread, but in practice the variations in detail design are legion, although they do have one thing in common. The adjustment of tool height is simple and quick, relying on a nut and lock-nut; once set correctly the tool can usually be removed, stored and replaced without needing to change anything.

Fig. 9.2 A low-price Quick Change Tool Post set, which seems at first sight to be a better alternative, but...

Fig. 9.3 The whole tool is made from light alloy and lacks a positive location.

Fig. 9.4 Light alloy again, and simply not strong or long lasting.

Each tool holder has a stud extending up from the top surface and this carries an adjuster nut that locates on the top surface of the central block, carried on the tool platform of the lathe. Tools are held in the holders by grub screws or set screws, often with hexagon socket heads, just like the more usual square toolpost. The differences arise when we come to securing the tool holder firmly in place on the central block, so that it can be removed and replaced with the cutting edge returning to its original position, sideways as well as upwards. Location can be by making the block and the holder to form matching dovetails or by providing V-grooves and ridges that fit closely together. The block may include a piston that is pushed outwards, a T-piece that is pulled inwards or a wedge that is moved downwards to finish the locating role.

In order to get really accurate location every time, the machining of the parts has to be very accurate, and for them to stand repeated use, they need to be made of tool steel, hardened and ground. As a result they are expensive. You need an accurate holder for every one of the turning tools you use regularly or there is little point in such a device. In consequence of the expense, many people have made extra holders themselves and sometimes the blocks as well, some expertly and others less well made: unless you buy new, and from a reliable source, you can never be sure what you are going to get. My advice, then, for those looking to invest in a QCTP, is to try to obtain a decent number of fully matching holders all at the same time, say at least six, and only to buy what you know to

Fig. 9.5 This block is a more expensive version, made from tool steel, ground to size, and with a positive repeat wedge lock.

Fig. 9.3 This holder, made to match the block in Fig. 9.5, is made from tool steel with ground surfaces – long lasting, accurate and firm.

Fig. 9.6 Another ground steel design, accurately made, with a piston lock.

Tool Holding for Milling

The discussions above about collets for holding work apply just as much to holding a milling cutter. The important details are that the tool is held firmly so that it cannot work its way loose, or slide out of place, and that it runs properly concentric with the axis of the machine. Collets of all the types discussed earlier should meet these requirements, as long as the holders and collets are undamaged and clean.

All this talk about collets might make you think that a drill chuck would serve just as effectively, but it won't. The milling operation applies a continuously rotating side load to the cutter, quite different from the end load of a twist drill, and this will cause the cutter to fidget in a drill chuck until it comes loose. A collet bears on almost the whole of the surface of the tool, whereas a drill chuck has three thin jaws and lots of empty space.

be a good reliable set. This is likely to mean that you need to see and handle what is on offer, to ensure that all the holders fit correctly. Make sure that you take with you the tool platform and post from your lathe and a note of the required cutting edge position (the height from the toolpost platform to the centre of the lathe mandrel), since some of the larger toolpost fittings do

not allow for the relatively low centre-height and high toolpost height of a small lathe. Those whose purses are not deep enough to buy a full set should not be tempted to try to make up a set piecemeal, or to buy unseen, but would be better advised to wait until they can save up, meanwhile making do with what they have.

10 Projects for Your Own Workholding Needs

STEEL SPACER BLOCKS FROM OFFCUTS

One of the first things you are likely to need when getting to grips with the potential of a new milling machine is a supply of metal to practise on, and as soon as you load up your nice new vice you are sure to need an accurate spacer, or more likely two. Both these needs can be met if you can acquire a selection of offcuts of bright mild steel. This material has the advantages that it is produced with a good surface finish and is fairly accurate in terms of flatness; the corners are sharp and the edges at right angles. If you don't have a local engineering firm who can help or a mate from your local model engineering club with some useful bits to get you started, try looking on the Web for material. If all else fails, you will have to order from a specialist supplier for the home engineering trade or visit a model engineering show. Packs of assorted sizes in lengths to suit the postal system can fill this need quite well. However you end up with offcuts, you will find that the bar ends are not square, or pretty, or even the lengths you need, but that can be corrected. The most useful products as spacers need to be properly flat on all faces, properly at right angles and, ideally, in pairs of the same thickness, width and length. This is how I would proceed with my box of offcuts.

First, we need to work out how to hold the workpieces so that the faces to be machined finish up properly at right angles to their remaining faces. Some can be clamped upright between the jaws of a machine vice, using an accurate square between the jaws to hold the block upright as the vice is tightened, so that a cutter can machine the top face. Then the work is turned over, checked for square again (it should be fine this time) and remachined with a light skim. This does not need the vice to be fixed and aligned with the X axis with precision, but it does need an accurate engineer's square that is thinner than the block you are working on, to set the edges vertical, and it needs a vice with an accurately flat surface between the jaws. Otherwise, blocks can be held flat in the vice (supported on spacers unless the vice is fairly small and low) so that the ends can be trimmed with the edge of a milling cutter moving in the Y direction. Of course, for this to succeed, the vice jaws do need to be set accurately in line with the X movement and at right angles to the Y. With any luck, there will be pairs of pieces, perhaps different lengths but the same width and the same thickness, ideally cut from the same stock, and these are exactly what we need for supporting work, on the table directly or in a vice. This will not be quite as accurate or as resistant to knocks as proper hardened and ground stock, but nowhere near as expensive and quite good enough to get you started.

One way to ensure that the widths do finish up exactly the same is to bolt the two slabs firmly together towards each end, or if you do not want to drill holes in the slabs for this, use a toolmaker's clamp and then, holding the pair's edges upwards and square in the vice, mill just enough off the top edge to clean up both edges. Then invert the pair over an accurate spacer in the vice and do the same to clear up the opposite edges in the same way, without disturbing the clamping pressure or undoing the bolts throughout the processing. Remember just before the final tightening of the vice to tap the workpieces downwards onto the locating surface with a plastic-faced mallet. You will get used to recognizing the solid noise produced when you tap on firmly located parts, quite distinct from the louder click when movement takes place. Again, this is likely to require an accurate spacer in the vice for the work to rest on, allowing room above the vice for the clamping arrangements, both ways round. Then remove the bolts or clamps and grip each slab separately using its newly machined edges in the vice, with

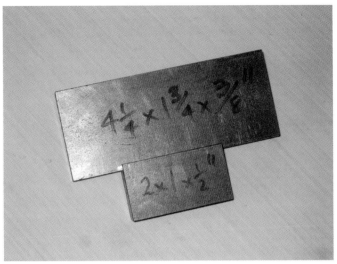

Fig. 10.1 Marker pen can identify block sizes until there is time for a more permanent solution.

no favours at all. If the vice is fitted with smooth jaws (see the next project) the grip against rotation can be reduced, so here is a tool that holds more firmly and is simple to make for a range of bar sizes. The material needed is a length of square bright steel bar and four small machine screws, nuts and penny washers; the tools you need are a drill and a range of bits, ideally a column drill (or even a vertical mill), a hacksaw and a file. The exact sizes depend on

the face horizontal (on accurate spacers again) and skim the ends with the mill so that they are smooth, flat and square to the edges. The object of this work is to equip yourself with pairs of blocks that can be used on their sides as supports for work held in a vice or in a similar position. Many parts need to be held up from the lowest surface between the jaws, but still parallel to this surface, pairs of blocks do the job well. If your vice is rather narrow, or you are not confident that the surface between the jaws is properly horizontal, use a pair of blocks clamped to the machine table on either side of the vice (using screws recessed into the top surfaces), so that the work can rest on them. Then machine the tops dead level while in position and the work resting on them, but held firm by the vice, so they will be held precisely.

Mark each of your new parts with the size and keep the pairs of spacers together and away from the general box of offcuts, so that they are not bruised on the important surfaces

and are still there when you next need them. Perhaps too, you could identify pairs as such by marking both parts with a letter or a number, using small punches or an engraving tool on the sides, rubbing down afterwards with emery to remove the burrs this creates. Alternatively, the dimensions can be etched into the surface. This marking method has the advantage that no burrs are produced, but the techniques are outside our remit under the work holding banner.

A ROUND-BAR HOLDER FOR TAPPING BAR AND SIMILAR TASKS

Whenever it is necessary to hold round bar for an operation, such as tapping or filing at the bench, difficulties can arise. Anyone who has ever done work on 'previously owned' machinery will be familiar with the checker marks left by holding parts, particularly round ones, in an engineer's bench vice. As a way of holding work this has a long history, but it does the appearance of the work

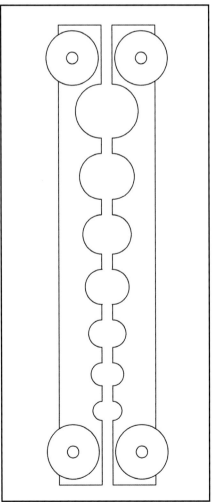

Fig. 10.2 A holder for round parts, ideal when holding parts in a bench vice for cutting threads and similar jobs.

the size of bar you are likely to need to hold and the length of your vice jaws. Cut two lengths of square bar slightly longer than your vice jaws and tidy the ends with a file. A hole drilled across each end of each bar will allow you to add screws and washers to overlap the bar edges as shown here. These washers are to locate the bars when held in the vice.

Decide on the range of bar sizes you are going to need to hold, perhaps 6, 8, 10 and 12mm, or ¼, ⁵⁄₁₆, ⅜, ⁷⁄₁₆ and ½in, and make a sketch to position each hole so that there is a reasonable clear space (say 6mm) between each hole. Hold the two prepared bars together with a strip of thick paper or thin card between them, mark the card with the hole centres using a soft pencil, for example. The bars need to be held really firmly together, so use a pair of toolmaker's clamps or vice grips at the ends. Then clamp the bars, still held together, in a drill vice or machine vice. The drilling of the holes is to be done in two stages, starting with a small hole to reduce the load on the finishing size. One of the larger holes should be completed first, a bar of this size (perhaps a bolt) clamped in place to avoid any tendency for the bars to move sideways during further drilling. The use of a card spacer should ensure that each of the finished holes is able to grip the appropriate size of bar really firmly, without making significant marks on it. If this is not the case, perhaps because your drill bits are not new and so not ground to exact dimensions, you can remove a small amount of metal from the inside faces of the bars. This tool will not give you a line of holes that are accurately at right

angles to the top face, unless you set it up very carefully, but for many purposes this is not vital. If you do need this accuracy, the holes should be bored in a mill and perhaps reamed to final size. For a really professional pair of bars, you might also mill away the outer faces by say 2 or 3mm to leave a location strip for the vice edges, instead of relying on bolts and washers overlapping the top surface of the jaws. If this is your intention, do this milling first so that the next operations are all based on the same locations.

PLAIN JAWS FOR BENCH VICES

For many work-holding tasks using a bench vice, the traditional grip marking of the jaws is an embarrassment. Soft jaws made from light-alloy angle, or faced with fibre, are a standard solution, but better results can be achieved by a more permanent change. What you can do depends on the facilities available, as well as what you need to hold. If you can get surface grinding done, it can be a simple matter to remove the jaw plates and have the surface markings ground off. Most vice jaws are too hard to machine using other methods. If the jaws come back with very sharp edges, use a strip of emery on a flat file to remove the edge just enough to eliminate the sharpness and refit the jaws using the original screws. Add washers to the screws if the grinding results in the screws being proud of the inside faces. Alternatively, new jaws to the same sizes, but without the offensive grip marks, can be made from bright mild steel slabs, or perhaps from light alloy or even brass. The only difficulty

I find with using metals softer than steel is the tendency for hard particles of swarf to embed themselves in the softer surface, resulting in marking of the workpiece, especially if that is also of a relatively soft material, such as light alloy. One answer is to make up two sets of jaws, reserving one set for finely finished work and using the other set for less critical day-to-day jobs.

BRIDGING BARS FOR T-SLOTS

This is a simple task, relying on drilling and tapping, sawing (which could be done with an angle grinder) and filing. The idea is to help to solve the problem that sometimes the slots in your mill table, or on the tool platform of your lathe, are not in the places where you need to add a clamp stud. If you only have a lathe, you can certainly make up a pair of bridge bars, but until you have a mill, you won't really have so much use for them, and in any event you won't yet know the critical dimensions, as mills do tend to vary widely. The dimensions you need are: the size and thread of your clamping set studs (often M8 or M10 for modern sets for use with modern machines, but other inch sizes are still around) and the distance between your T-slots, which we shall call D. Measure them from edge to edge of one of the 'lands' on your table and across the width of one slot, and add these together to give D, the centre-to-centre distance.

This gives you the distance between the plain drilled fixing holes in your bar and their size. The material you need is a flat bar of steel at least 2D + 50mm long, and about 25mm wide by 12mm thick.

Fig. 10.3 Measuring the pitch of the bed slots.

This will make two bridging bars. Bright mild steel bar would be ideal, but black bar will serve too, although it is not so smooth or so pretty and never has the free-cutting character that is so helpful in some grades of bright bar. Mark out a centre line on the length of the flat side of the bar and scribe a line across the end at the same distance from the edge. This gives you the first plain hole position, so mark it with a centre pop. Measure distance D from this point and mark a second centre pop on the centre line. Now do exactly the same starting from the other end of the bar. Now you need to decide where the new clamp bar location is going to be of most use: perhaps midway between the ends or more towards one end? You could even make one of each. When you have decided, mark another centre pop on the centre line in the chosen positions. Three drill bits will be needed, one the clearance size of the studs, which is not a critical dimension and another for the tapping size of the studs, which needs to be accurate and the third as a pilot for the two bigger holes. For M10 studs the tapping size is 8.5mm, for M8 studs, 6.7mm and for M6, 5.3mm. It might mean buying special drills, but they are sure to be useful for other tasks too. In addition you will also need a taper tap, 10 × 1.5mm for M10, for M8 8 × 1.25mm and for M6 6 × 1mm. None of these should cost much more than a pint of ale, as a pilot drill a 2.5mm or 3mm or ⅛in would be useful. If times really are hard, you can modify the design slightly by using plain holes throughout and making extra room for a nut below the bridge. This method avoids buying a tap and a tapping drill, but needs spacers between the table and the bar; extra wide washers and plain nuts of the next size up can be handy for this.

To use the lathe for the next operations, you need to hold drill bits in turn in the headstock and leave the tailstock open so that a drill point can pass into it. The pilot drill goes in the three-jaw chuck, or a collet held in the taper, or a drill chuck in the mandrel, it doesn't matter which. Set the speed appropriately, that is fairly slow, and move the tailstock so there is about 20mm between the face of the tailstock hole and the end of the drill. Lock the tailstock in position. Start the lathe, holding the bar in your left hand so that its far end rests flat against the tailstock with the centre pop in line with the rotating drill. Now use your right hand to wind the tailstock towards the chuck and make sure that, as contact is made, the drill enters the centre pop mark. Keep the bar flat against the tailstock and continue winding slowly, so that

Fig. 10.4 A bridge piece that allows a clamping stud to be positioned between the slots..

the drill does its work and makes a hole that is square to the face of the bar. Be aware that as the drill breaks through it will tend to snatch the bar briefly, so brace yourself for this. Back off the tailstock, remove the bar and do the same to produce all the other pilot holes. Of course, if you have a column drill you might prefer to use that for these pilot holes, or even a hand-held drill, as the accuracy of these clearance holes is not critical. Then replace the pilot drill with the largest size for the job (that is, the clearance size for your clamping studs) and drill the two end holes and the two central holes in the same way. Where we do need to be more careful is in drilling and tapping the two remaining holes that are to take studs. These tapped holes need to be accurately at right angles to the face of the bar, so a hand-held drill is ruled

out. Instead we might rely on the lathe again or a column drill. It is possible, with care, to hold a tap vertically in the drill chuck, with the work clamped in a vice on the drill table, or even hand-held over a through hole to give the tap clearance. As the tap is turned by hand to start the thread, the drill handle is pressed, very lightly, downwards to keep track of the tapping process. A better idea is to hold a sleeve, a simple length of tube, in the drill chuck and use a tap-holding chuck mounted on a cylindrical extension to slide within the tube.

This tap holder is another exercise you can make yourself – a bought-out drill chuck is fitted to a threaded adaptor, which is a simple turning job. However you start the tap, use hand power only – do not be tempted to try to cut these threads under power. Once

the tap has properly started to cut, you can loosen the tap holder and remove the bar, tap still in place, to the bench where you can continue and finish the tapping, holding the bar in a bench vice. To avoid screwing a stud in too far when using the bar, so marking the machine table, bruise the lower face of the thread using a blunt cold chisel, as recommended when making T-nuts (*see* Chapter 5). Run a smooth file across the bottom face to remove the burrs this creates. Finally, cut the two bars to length, holding the bar in a bench vice with protection on the jaws, perhaps using a hacksaw or a thin-blade angle grinder and file a radius, or chamfers, on the ends. This not merely gives a neat finish, it also allows clearance against other parts when in use. This exercise is an example of the simplest form of work holding where the necessary accuracy comes from the bar being held flat

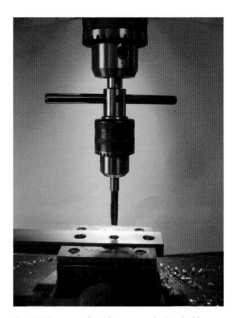

Fig. 10.5 To start a thread square to the bar, hold a tap-holder in a column drill as a support, turning the tap by hand (and never under power).

Fig. 10.6 Knocking
down the lowest
thread to stop a stud
passing right through
and locking on the
table surface.

*Fig. 10.7 The home-made bridge bar, tidied up and
ready for use.*

against the tailstock nose or the drill platform, the work is prevented from rotating by holding the bar as a handle. Now you see why the operation of cutting to length is left to the last.

HOLDING WORK SO THAT NOTHING PROJECTS ABOVE IT

Tasks such as fly-cutting require the tool to move over a relatively large area, so conventional milling clamps, which hold the work from above, will get in the way. This is a particular problem where planers and shapers are commonly used in heavy engineering; our grandfathers, of course, worked out solutions. Unfortunately this method, relying on stops fitted into outer slots in the table, doesn't quite work for the smaller mill, as the table is not wide enough to carry more than three T-slots. The answer is to make up clamps to hold in the T-slots against forces in line with the slots, rather than at right angles to them. The side force in this method is likely to be fairly high, so to increase the friction available the provision of two holding down bolts for each clamp is recommended. If the milling or similar operation is likely to produce a large side force on the workpiece, it will be helpful to add a further stop on movement of the work in that direction, such as a simple block or slab clamped with further T-bolts. This will prevent any overloading of the relatively thin angled clamp bars, leading to their failure and loosening of the work. The clamping bars I have used for this method are home made from bright mild steel 6 × 30mm, with a gentle bend, with one end ground to an edge of about 1mm. This works well for light alloy workpieces.

To hold a steel slab in the same way the clamps should be made of spring steel, to the same dimensions, hardened and tempered at the sharper end. The clamp needs to be harder than the work. Some marking of the workpiece is usual where the clamps bear, so if these faces need to be immaculate, you might need to reconsider the order in

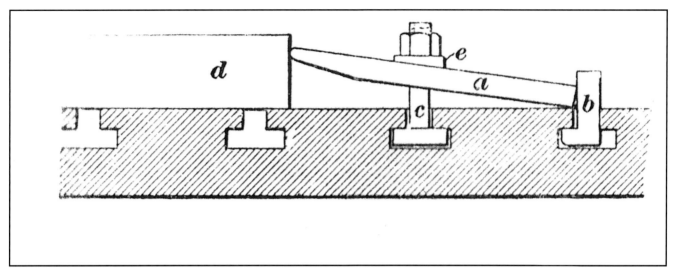

Fig. 10.8 Designed for a planing machine with a wide table, low clamps like these need a special thrust block for use on a small mill.

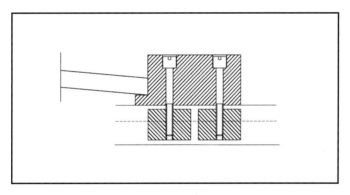

Fig. 10.9 Cross-section of a suitable block for the low clamps. Two T-nuts and two socket screws give strength.

MAKING A TOOL FOR SCREW SLOTTING

If you only have a few screws to slot, you can hold a row of a few screws in a modified vice. Replace the standard steel jaw inserts of your machine vice with light-alloy slabs. Grooves are made in the slabs to hold the screws ready for slotting, so choose an alloy if you can that is known to be easy to

which the machining and finishing is carried out.

machine with a good finish. How the vice is to be held in practice depends on how you will cut the slots. If your mill head can be moved so that the arbor is horizontal, you can use a machine saw mandrel held in a collet, moving the table (and vice with the workpieces) in the Y direction beneath it. If you have a horizontal mill, it is easy to add a saw blade to the arbor and slot in the X direction. If you only have a lathe, the job is still possible, with the saw blade in its mandrel held in the chuck and the work mounted on the saddle so that it

can pass below the saw or if there is no room to do this, fit the vice to a milling adaptor plate with a vertical traverse. In each case, you need to pass a row of part-finished screws past a rotating saw blade, not the easiest of jobs to arrange on a lathe, especially as you need to ensure above all that your hands must not come into contact with the whirling teeth. As for the modification of the machine vice, the size of the slabs is not critical, ideally about 6mm thick and wide enough to completely fill the vice jaws with a bit over. Cut two pieces to fit the jaw space, drill and tap for the standard holding screws; if these screws now protrude inside the jaws, add a washer or two below their heads to prevent this.

Fit the vice to the bed of your mill or on the lathe, so that the jaws are exactly in line with the movement needed for slotting. An easy way to do this is to trap a straight edge (lightly) between the jaws so that it sticks out on both sides, use a DTI or a wobbler in place

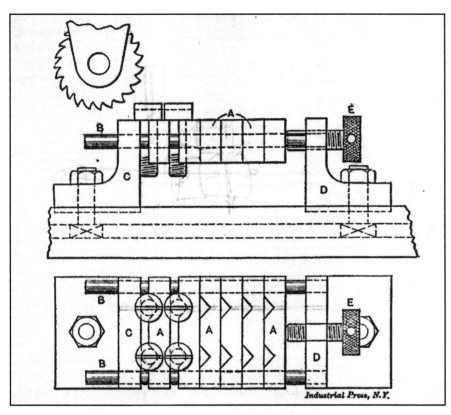

Fig. 10.10 Screw-head slotting needs patience, or a set-up like this sketch from about 1910.

the finish or exact sizes of the grooves is the problem, it may be necessary to turn the alloy slabs over and start again, remachining the holes using a smaller drill and finishing off with an end mill to take out the final shaving. The spacing of the grooves does not matter, what is important is their alignment on which depends the centring of the slots in the finished products. Once the process is finished, it should be possible to save the grooved plates for future use whenever the thread details remain the same.

While researching for this volume, I came across a design from about 1900, or perhaps even earlier, which ensures that each screw is held with exactly the same amount of grip. To produce good results however, some really accurate repeat machining is required, so I do not suggest that this is the first project you undertake. Anyone with regular batches of similar screws to slot, amounting to more than half a dozen or so, may find that this tool is worth making up. The tool comprises a pair of end plates like small angle plates, which are bolted to the table of the milling machine. One of the angle plates also has a central adjusting screw. Also carried by holes in the plates are two round steel bars for which silver steel would be ideal. On these bars are strung a series of screw carriers, made from square bar, each with a pair of V-grooves on one side. The screws to be slotted are placed in pairs in each block, they are held firm by a central screw in one of the end plates. It looks really simple, but there are problems unless your accuracy is beyond reproach. The heads of the screws need to be level – parallel with

of the saw mandrel to check that no variation is noted as the vice is traversed across, in other words that both ends of the straight edge are in line with the movement of the table. To ensure that the slots in the screws are all exactly in line, we need to make the grooves for the screws with the vice held, and moved, in the same way as the slots are to be cut. Clamp the vice up tight onto a thick strip of card or a few strips of paper. This is to ensure that the cutter used to make the grooves follows the join and does not veer off into the alloy on either side. Select a drill of about the tapping size of the screw threads and hold it in the machine using a collet, if possible, rather than a drill chuck, giving less overhang and better centring. Position

the table so that the drill is exactly in line with the card and drill a series of holes in the jaw-plates, deep enough to hold the full length of the newly made screws. Use plenty of lubricant and a sharp drill, do not allow swarf to accumulate in the drill flutes or the finish and size will both suffer. This should produce a line of holes in which the new screws can be gripped for the slotting operation. If the screws to be slotted are brass, it will help to tighten the vice first on a row of steel screws of the same thread exactly, this will form a witness of the thread in the alloy and avoid any distortion of the new screws. The difficulty you may find with this method is that with a row of screws all held in the same jaws, some screws will not be held as tightly as others. If the surface on which the tool is fixed – or the slots will not be the same depth in all the screws. This means that the bars must be exactly level, so must the surfaces of the blocks, which means that the holes must all be a precision fit on the bars. The V-notches also need precision – if they are uneven in depth the blocks will tilt and jam on the bars, the V-slots need to be accurately positioned in relation to the bar locations, or the screws will not be properly in line. The length of the V-grooves in the blocks is also important, as unless the screws go well past the centre point, the blocks will tilt as the system is clamped up, the screws will not be held firm and the threads may be damaged. This seems to me like a job for which a properly thought-out jig is required, so that the holes in the bars can be machined accurately and the V-slots cut while they are firmly located on hardened pegs to fit both holes.

EXTRA PARTS FOR YOUR CLAMPING KIT

These parts will help to make a clamping system more effective and reliable, as they will ensure that clamping loads are applied centrally rather than at the edges of components, and any minor tilting or out-of-flatness is properly accommodated. The principle used in solving these problems is to interpose a curved surface that will allow the load to be spread evenly when the clamped surfaces themselves are not parallel. The accompanying illustrations show the parts involved and some of them in use.

Fig. 10.11 Dome ends from coach bolts and slices of curved steel can improve your clamping system.

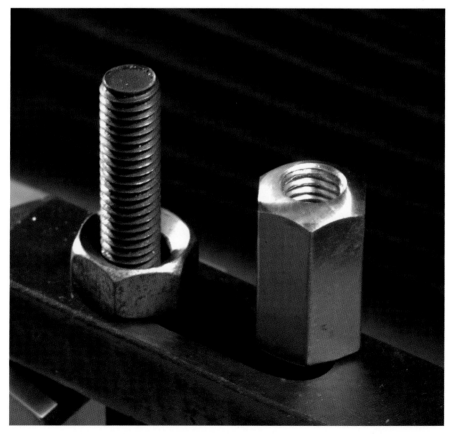

Fig. 10.12 A curved hollow in the thick washer and a radius on the deep nut even out the load on a clamping bar.

Fig. 10.13 The handrail section and domed nut system combined.

Part A: Made simply from the smallest size of 'handrail steel' – not half-round exactly, but with a curved face; a short length (200 or 300mm) is all you will need. Cut off pieces a bit wider than the clamps in your kit, remove the burrs and rub the flat side even flatter on a sheet of emery so that all traces of black scale are removed from the flat face. Do the same with the curved face. That's all; the tool is finished. In use rest the flat surface on your work, or on the part to be held down, and add the clamp resting on the curved surface. It may be necessary to turn the new curved part a few degrees so that the contact with the clamp is along a line all the way across, not merely at one side. If the handrail section is too big for your scale of working, you can achieve the same result by slicing a segment from a round mild steel, or light alloy, bar of an appropriate diameter for your needs. At the smallest sizes, use can be made of the extruded light-alloy strip (like a miniature handrail section) used to cover the joints in traditional coachwork. This can be obtained from specialist vintage vehicle suppliers.

Part B: Cut off the dome and square from a coach bolt, tidy the cut edges and that is all there is to it. The dome part is useful when you need to add a clamp to hold down a part (such as a clamp bar) with a slot or hole into which the square will fit, so that the load is applied across the bar and not just at one side. Select bolts if you can that are plain on the top; or if you can only find those with lettering, remove it with a file so that the surface is reasonably evenly domed. If the coach bolt is the same size as your clamping studs, save the threaded offcut, having removed the burrs from the cut end, as it could be useful whenever a low clamp is needed.

Parts C and D: A nut and washer with matching male and female radiused faces, for use where the stud is not exactly at right angles to the clamp on which it bears. There are two ways to make these, one that is accurate but fiddly and requires special tooling, the other much simpler and quicker to make, but not quite a proper radius in reality. Both start with a long nut as supplied in a clamping kit for joining two studs together (widely available on the Web) and a plain nut of the next thread size up. Long nuts are used because they are much easier to hold firmly in a chuck and the threads are more likely to be square to the hexagon. For the cheap and cheerful versions, hold the long nut in the three-jaw chuck of the lathe so that about 6mm protrudes. Turn a chamfer on the outer end in three stages, at about 65, 60 and 55 degrees from the axis, so that you have a blunt end with three angles. This is what has to make do as the basis of a radius, so use a strip of medium emery on a file as the nut rotates to round off the angles evenly all round. Finish with fine emery in the same way. This is the 'male' component finished. The 'female' part is a thick washer with a clearance hole, made perhaps by drilling out the threads of an ordinary nut of the next

Fig. 10.14 As the sharp tool rotates quickly and the work slowly, a spherical surface is produced.

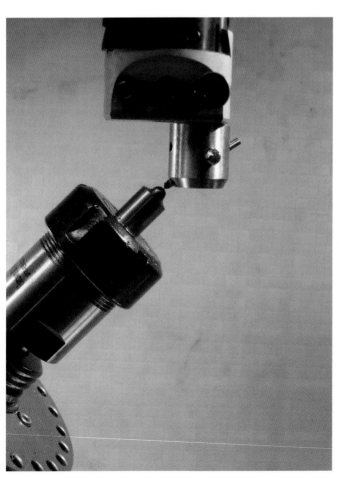

size up. Don't leave the hole too small or it will not be able to swivel on the matching radius, which is the whole object of this exercise. Use the same lathe set-up and position the nut square against the face of the chuck. If necessary use a spacer so that the outer edge of the nut protrudes about 1 to 2mm. Drill out the thread and turn a 30-degree chamfer in the inside of the outer face. The nut is likely to have a chamfer of about 45 degrees as manufactured: all you need is to remake it at 30 degrees and deep enough to remove all of the flat outer face. In use, the washer goes over the stud and rests on the clamp, with the new chamfer upwards; and

Fig. 10.15 The same set-up exactly, with the tool now at the top of the sphere.

the nut, rounded end downwards, is tightened down onto it. These parts do not have proper spherical surfaces, but in practice they will still allow the self-aligning process that ensures that whenever the parts are not at right angles, a condition which is very likely in practice, properly secure clamping is the result.

Truly spherical surfaces on the same components require the use of more specialized tooling; one answer is a radius attachment for a lathe, another is a dividing head (or a rotary table) on a mill. Mine were made with a dividing head set on a milling table at about 25 degrees from the vertical, with the radius on the long nuts generated by a boring head with the cutting edge set inwards. Boring cutters made for boring heads are not normally available that way round, so I had to make one specially, with its own tool holder to fit my half-inch boring head. The larger-than-standard nuts, used for simplicity instead of making thick washers from bar, were drilled out on the lathe and then hollowed at one end on the same dividing head settings with a small fly-cutter machining across the diameter (and rotating the normal way). In both cases, the mill was set running and the dividing head was rotated slowly until the cutter had done its work all the way round. The fly-cutter was set to cut at the same radius as that of the boring head, at about twice the outer diameter of the nut-washer, but remember when measuring that, in the case of the boring head, the cutter needs to cut on the inside edge, while the fly-cutter cuts on the outside. The cutting diameter within the boring head can be difficult to determine, so use it to mill down a couple of millimetres into a block of MDF and you can measure, and adjust and remeasure, the diameter produced. The feed was produced by moving the milling head down about 0.25mm at a time while continuing to rotate the work slowly by turning the handle on the dividing head or rotary table, until the radius occupied the whole of the outer surface. If you prefer to use a dedicated radius attachment for your lathe, the same results can be achieved, but as these devices come in various styles and operating methods, the advice is to follow the instructions with the kit and all should be well. The finish required on the surfaces does not have to be perfect; you will find that after they have been in use a few times, the relatively soft steel of ordinary steel nuts becomes smoother in any case, where it has been subject to the force of tightening.

The same technique is used to produce the ball-ended centres suggested for turning tapered work between centres. In this case, the ball is produced on the end of a soft centre or a short cylindrical bar of silver steel to be carried in a collet in the lathe mandrel or the tailstock, it needs to be both accurately centred and finely finished. This, of course, should have a smaller finished diameter than the washers above, 6mm or less. Before making the ball itself, turn the end to a cylinder with a length and diameter just larger than the design size of the finished sphere, with an undercut so that the cutter does not have much to remove from the back edge of the sphere where it will not be in contact with the centre

in use. In reality, you don't need an undercut at all; a dome-ended cylinder of the right size (to fit within the work centre) will serve perfectly well. Use a fine feed and plenty of cutting oil as the required size is approached. To improve the finish further, spin the result in the lathe at a fairly high speed and use fine emery and oil, followed by a finer abrasive, such as T-cut on a small piece of soft cloth.

TOOLS FOR ACCURATE LOCATION AGAINST A CHUCK BODY

The outer face of any chuck is manufactured with a flat surface at right angles to the axis on which it is mounted. This face can provide an accurate endwise location for a cylindrical workpiece held within the jaws for further work, but only if the hole through the chuck is not too large. Sometimes though, the face of the

chuck body can become scored around the central hole, especially when the chuck is used for boring operations (always by a previous owner, of course), this removes the precision needed as a locating face. A range of simple tooling can be made up to overcome these difficulties. In each case the starting point is a disc or washer of metal that is properly flat and even in thickness. Ordinary commercial wide washers are usually fairly good in this respect ('repair washers' or 'penny washers' are most useful), as long as there are no burrs from the production process around the inner or outer edges. For really accurate facing, the locating plate could usefully be made from 'gauge plate', which is steel ground accurately flat on both faces. This means extra work though, as the steel is a lot harder to cut than mild steel, even in its annealed state. There is no need to harden the finished part though, as

Fig. 10.16 The rough surface between the jaws prevents it forming a reliable location.

Fig. 10.17 Drop a spacer like this into place and even small parts are stopped accurately.

blue (or anything similar, such as black grease or lipstick) and lay the chuck face down on a piece of paper. The marks produced will be your guide for the removal of metal from your washer. This can be done using a hacksaw and files or, if you need some practice with more fancy kit, on a rotary table on the mill. If you are really in a hurry, an angle grinder with a thin disc will get you started. Do be careful to avoid bending the washer arms though, as this will prevent the finished part from sitting properly flat on the chuck face. Keep the chuck handy at the same settings as you remove metal, so that you can try the fit, allowing some slack so that the chuck can be tightened without interference from the washer. In reality, you could do exactly the same processes without needing a central hole on a plain flat piece of steel (or hard brass or light alloy), but washers provide a handy starting point and the hole does allow you to keep a selection of such parts handy on a nail, ready for future applications.

the pressure on the washer in use is not going to be a problem. The finished washer must fit flat against the face of the chuck, modification of the washer involves cutting away metal that would interfere with the position of the vice jaws. This makes a part that is Y shaped for a three-jaw chuck and X shaped for a four-jaw. The dimensions depend on the details of the chuck and the position of the jaws when holding the intended workpiece, but the required cutaways do not need to be particularly accurate as long as the jaws can still move freely. A simple way to proceed starts with the chuck off the lathe, adjusted to the size needed. Smear the outermost faces of the jaws lightly with engineer's

Fig. 10.18 For parts that are to be drilled or bored, a tubular end is needed. This stop is machined from a soft MT2 fitting.

Another way to solve this problem is rather more complicated, but has the benefit of being more readily adjustable and of suiting any chuck you might need to use. It relies on making something to fit in the headstock mandrel and to extend far enough into the middle of the chuck to be useful. If there is a taper in your headstock mandrel, then you can use a collet to match, a drawbar to tighten it and a flanged rod (shaped very like a valve from a car engine) to locate within it. Make the head of the flange properly flat and almost, but not quite, the diameter of the part to be held and machined. This allows the head of the tool to fit within the vice jaws as it is tightened on the work. If the part to be machined has a central hole to be drilled or bored or tapped in the lathe, make the flange from a soft mandrel with a counterbore, so that the cutting tool has room to pass within it.

Machine the end to fit within the bore of the chuck, if necessary, and bore out the same end to leave a flat-ended tube about 3 or 4mm thick. This flat face will act as the stop for the workpiece and the hole allows for drilling and boring operations right through the work.

The adjustment to get the positioning correct should be carried out before the drawbar is tight, then nip up the drawbar and it will all remain firm in the same place exactly, whether the chuck itself is open or closed. Repetition work becomes easier this way. Accurate positioning of the stop can present problems, as the tightening of the drawbar can tend to pull the collet, and the stop held within it, inwards. To avoid this, use the largest collet you can fit (so, for an MT2 taper use ½in or 12mm) and

Fig. 10.19 On the left, a soft fitting as bought; on the right the same part has been counterbored so a drill can pass into it.

make up a sleeve of that diameter with an internal thread to take a long screw as the flange fitting. Another option is to use a plain sleeve and a loose flange-piece threaded to take a nut and simply push it into place as the workpiece is inserted into the chuck.

FACING A NUT TRUE TO THE THREADS

I am not a great believer in shake-proof washers, and I regard spring washers as not much better. How then, can we stop things coming undone from

Fig. 10.20 An MT collet can hold a bolt or similar part as an adjustable end stop for small-diameter bar.

vibration? I start from advice given long ago by a Service Engineer at Norton motorcycles, who pointed out that the single-cylinder Manx Norton, a racing machine not known for its smoothness, did not include a single spring or shake-proof washer. It relied, he said, on properly flat surfaces and properly true nuts and bolts, properly tightened. Machining your fastenings so that the bearing surfaces are flat and square to the axis should be relatively easy, but what about bought-in components? Mass-produced nuts are the worst offenders, in my experience, with threads that can be way out of line with the faces and the flats. The answer is not to lock two nuts onto a true-running thread and face the end, as there is always clearance in the thread and no certainty that the result will be much better, as any out-of-square of one nut is carried over to the other. We need to ensure that the nut is centralized on the thread, and only on the thread, without any tilting of the central bore, even if both faces are on the skew. Only then can we machine the face really square to the thread. Various methods can be used, each relying on an extra part, or two, and any of which can be made in a morning.

Method 1: This uses a pair of washers that are flat on the outsides but matching part-spheres where they contact each other. In addition, the centre hole needs to be larger than normal, allowing the washers to swivel as a load is applied. You will, I hope, have noticed this idea when we were covering clamping systems. This time, you might need to work on nuts that are smaller, or larger, than your clamping kit, so the first job is to make up a pair of a suitable size. To carry the nut that needs to be accurate, set up a bolt or threaded bar in the lathe to run true, perhaps using a collet or a four-jaw chuck. It can be difficult to use a DTI to check the truth against a thread surface, so use a flat-ended or flat-faced tool in the toolpost aligned with the crests of the thread, use a bright light to check how the gap varies as the chuck is turned by hand. Use an uncorrected off-the-shelf nut on the thread, add the pair of fancy part spherical washers and when you tighten the workpiece nut against them the washers will swivel so that all the load is applied by the threads. To be sure, roll one washer around in your fingers as you tighten the nut, this will help to ensure that the centralizing is complete. As a result, the nut thread is held firmly all the way round by the central thread, as any tilt in the end-load is evened out by rotation of the spherical washers.

If the nut is a special, perhaps of a finer thread than standard, extra nuts or bolts for holding purposes are ruled out, so you might have to undertake a thread-cutting exercise in order to make a mandrel to hold the work. In this case, before you make the mandrel, make up a thick washer with a bore to fit over the thread and face off the outer surface while the part is in the chuck. Turn the part end to end and the opposite face should be machined as one side of the part spherical pair. This part can then be slid over the newly cut thread, without disturbing it in the chuck, with the true-faced surface resting against the chuck jaws and the fancy part spherical outer surface

Fig. 10.21 To locate a nut concentric with its threads, a double-bevelled thick washer can be used like this.

forms the location for its partner. As the precious nut is tightened, the fancy washers will swivel round, as previously described, removing any tendency to angle the nut.

Method 2: The same result can be achieved by using a different style of fancy washer between two plain ones. The fancy washer is machined on its faces to leave a radial ridge on both sides, these ridges are at right angles. Making such a washer from bar is not easy, but it can be done if you cut a fine thread inside the washer, which clearly needs to be several millimetres thick to allow you to hold it safely and locate it on the end of a threaded mandrel. You could use an off-the-shelf nut for this, as long as you have a thread as a mandrel on which it can be carried. Two flats need to be cut or perhaps ground, or even filed, at an angle on each face, leaving a thin ridge between them. Then the washer is inverted on the mandrel and the next pair of flats finishes the work. The flats do not need to be at exactly the same angle: what is required is that the line where they join runs across the middle of the washer and is at right angles to the one on the other face.

Method 3: This is a further variation in which the fancy washer is made from a thick steel washer with a central hole just big enough to go over the thread and four short steel rivets. This washer is drilled with four holes to take steel rivets with domed heads. The holes are countersunk alternately, so that two opposite are countersunk and the two between them are countersunk

Fig. 10.22 Alternatively, use a washer fitted with rivets or grub screws.

Fig. 10.23 The four rivet heads allow the washer to tilt; the outer nut tightens on the threads without tipping itself.

on the other side. Rivets are fixed in the holes by cutting them flush and lightly spreading the cut end into the countersink, with the domed head held in a rivet set or on a block of lead. The result is a washer with two domes each side, opposite each other and at right angles to those on the other side – just what we need to ensure that when trapped between nuts, even if the nuts are tapped out of line, the load is carried centrally on the threads.

If you don't have any rivets to hand, an alternative method is to drill and tap the four holes at the same radius, two on a diameter and two exactly between them. Four short cone-pointed grub screws are added, adjusted so the points stick out equally each side, and set in place with thread-lock, with two points on one side and two on the other. This washer is then trapped between two nuts, just as with the rivet method, and each of these provides the self-adjusting tilting mechanism and avoids the fairly complex operation of machining washers at an angle. You might use 5mm grub screws and 5mm thick washers for threads of 10mm or above, or perhaps rather smaller for a small thread size. It isn't critical exactly how far the grub screws stick out, as long as they are spaced on radii at right angles. If you are concerned that the points will damage the surface of the nut, then use a thin plain washer to take the direct load. To help with this if you have doubts, the plain washer can be provided with dimples or small holes into which the points of the screws can be located on assembly.

FACEPLATE ADJUSTING SCREWS

These can be used to clamp in faceplate slots and assist with centralizing parts (and for holding large diameter parts lightly). Centralizing a part on a faceplate can involve a lot of tapping this way and that, but this can be eased with the help of a set of tools that are easy to make with a mill. These parts work best with a faceplate that has eight radial slots, as almost all do. Four slots are used to clamp the workpiece, the remaining four will be used for these tools. Toolroom accuracy is not needed to make these parts and the whole job might take a morning. Check the width of your faceplate slots – a 10mm clamp stud will usually leave a small clearance, but some smaller lathes might only take 8mm or 6mm studs. You will need some bright steel

bar, round or square, big enough to overlap the faceplate slots: 20mm or 25mm bar will usually be about right. As round bar is easier to find than square, these details are based on using it; if square bar is to hand, make the needed adjustments, with a milling vice in place of the V-blocks, for example. Four similar fittings will be needed. In order to make them in pairs, cut two lengths of bar each about 50mm long. Face both ends of both bars, drill and tap both ends for clamping studs. The depth of the tapped hole needs to be about the width of the stud or perhaps a little more, not less. Then screw in a short stud at both ends; ideally studs for this could be made from bolts with the heads cut off. Clamp down each bar in V-blocks on the mill table, resting the clamping bars on the studs, so that the whole length of the bar is accessible.

Fig. 10.24 The first stage in making faceplate locator blocks.

If no V-blocks are to hand, a machine vice can be used, with the bar held up on two identical spacers to bring the surface above the vice edges. Mill a flat the length of the top face, about the width of the studs, mark the mid-point of this face with a centre punch and use a centre held in a collet to start two holes centrally in this surface, each about 8mm away from the centre punch mark.

Reposition the bar so it is supported by the studs resting in the V-blocks, with a clamp on the mid-point. Drill through the centre drillings with tapping size for the adjusters and start a tap in each hole, removing it before the table is reached. If you are using a machine vice, the whole job of drilling and tapping can be completed without releasing the work, otherwise it will cause a delay while the horizontal position of the flat is restored. The tapping can now be completed holding the bar in a bench vice.

My preference is to use M6 socket screws as adjusters. They are 1mm thread pitch, so measuring any adjusting movement is easy, since one full turn is 1mm of movement, but set screws with hexagon heads may be easier to find than socket screws with a full thread. The small size allows the adjusters to be fairly close to the faceplate surface too.

Do not worry about providing a locating tab to hold the bar in the slot of the faceplate so that the block sits square and snug in the slot when in position. Flat ends will work well and holding the block in place while the nut is tightened can be done using the adjusters. In practice, the slots in the

Fig. 10.25 A pair of finished blocks – you will need four like this.

faceplate are likely to be cast rather than machined, so of a varying width, and this is not, in any case, a tool needing to be really tight. All that is needed now is to separate the two ends of each bar, using the centre pop marks as a guide. The job can be done in a few seconds with an angle grinder or a few minutes with a hacksaw. If you really need to, it can even be done in several more minutes (in my experience, at least) by setting up the lathe and parting off.

Fig. 10.26 In use, the locators fit in slots between the main clamps for the work and simplify centralization.

Do use the lathe to tidy up the ends though, and chamfer the corners to remove burrs neatly.

In use, the work is held by clamps through four of the radial slots in the faceplate, these adjusters are fitted to the four alternate slots, with socket screws fitted in each adjusting thread, bearing lightly against the workpiece. This allows the adjusters to be used to centralize the workpiece as the faceplate is turned by hand and the selected surface is clocked using a DTI.

The main clamps should be nipped up only lightly, allowing movement of the adjusters to achieve the required centralization. Then the clamps can be properly tightened, a check is made to ensure that nothing has moved in the process and the adjusters then removed completely so that machining can be carried out. Alternatively, if there is room for them, the adjusters can remain in place as this can allow the workpiece to be removed for other operations and replaced in the same position to be finished off.

A SIMPLE STOP FOR A MACHINE VICE

We have earlier seen how a clamp kit can be used to make a stop for work in a machine vice (*see* Chapter 5). It can be handy for some jobs to attach such a stop to the vice itself, rather than to the bed of the machine. Most machine vices have the separate steel jaw-plates held in place by hexagon socket screws. This provides an ideal attachment for a stop system and avoids having to add extra holes or other modification to the vice itself. Measure the separation of

Fig. 10.27 *These simple parts are all you need to add an adjustable stop to a machine vice.*

Fig. 10.28 *Trap the drilled bar with longer jaw screws and spacing washers, the stop block can be added at either end.*

the screws (mine are at 68mm centres exactly). We need a bar to locate on these screws, with extra holes to suit short or longer work pieces, so the decision is made to have a row of holes at 34mm centres. Black steel bar is used, 6mm thick by 25mm and a length of 230mm gives room for seven holes. None of these dimensions is critical, except (obviously) that the holes need to fit the screw centres. You can make the bar longer or shorter depending on the sizes of component you are machining. The rest of the kit comprises two longer bolts (or screws) to replace the originals and a pair of spacers to fit into the counterbores for the original screw heads.

Make the spacers the same length and the bar will sit in line with the jaws. The actual stop I use is a short piece of ¾in bright bar, drilled across for a tommy bar and tapped at the end for a short machine screw. If I find for a future job that I need more variation in position, I can mill flats on this bar and add a through hole, so that an adjuster bolt and nut can be added. The spare holes can also be used to add a plate to locate on the work in a higher or lower position. By making all the holes at 34mm centres, the bar can be fitted in any of five different positions sideways.

KITS FOR MAKING TOOLS

Among the kits available for making models are some that allow you to make tooling for work-holding tasks. These can be very useful if you are not sure what you want for a particular operation or are unsure about sizes,

or design details, or even if you are a long way from a ready source of the necessary metal sections and other useful bits and pieces. Here are some examples.

Hemingway Offset Tailstock

The name Hemingway is well known in the UK as a specialist in this area. Their Set-Over Centre is intended for taper turning without moving the tailstock from its central position, it offers a useful example for us. What you get is a box of parts, an excellent instruction sheet and full-size working drawings. Not only do you get the sizes for everything, the process is explained and the ways in which the finished product should be put to use. The finished device has an MT taper forming a T with a slotted strip of steel. Sliding in the slots is a similar strip carrying a

centre, the position of this centre can be adjusted away from the central position by thumbscrews and then held firmly in place by machine screws. In the box are an MT tapered arbor with a soft outer end to be machined to carry the crossbar, the two slabs of bright mild steel to make the crossbar and the slide that it carries, a decent length of silver steel for the new centre and the adjusters, and the socket screws and grub screw. The machining needed is not too complex, but it does cover a range of skills. The crossbar and slider need to be machined with matching grooves on the meeting faces, with tapped holes in the bar and shouldered slots in the slider. The taper arbor is to be threaded on the soft end to match the crossbar and a centre made to fit a similar hole in the slide. This leaves the adjuster screws to be turned, screw-cut and knurled. The threads specified

Fig. 10.29 A typical Hemingway kit. This one is number HK 1760/1761 for an adjustable offset centre for taper turning.

Fig. 10.30 The 3D view of the finished taper turning tool. HEMINGWAY KITS

and supplied are metric, which makes sense, with BSF alternatives detailed for those with more old-style taps than up-to-date versions. The dimensions on the drawings though, are in good old-fashioned inches and fractions, which go back, I suspect, to the original 1955 design. My suggestion for younger readers (at least) would be to spend an hour converting everything on the drawing to millimetres, with an eye for those dimensions that are particularly critical. In this case, that means not very much: although the two sliding parts do need to fit accurately together for the adjustment to work, most of the other dimensions need only to be followed to a millimetre or so.

If this idea appeals to you, here is another example from the same source that also helps to solve a work-holding problem. Full details of the supplier can be found at the end of the volume.

Balancing Stand for Lathe Faceplate Assembly etc.

This is going to be another tool that is simple to make. Nothing fancy, no elaborate, super accurate machining, no big bill for special parts. It's not a device to win prizes perhaps, but down to earth and functional. What I am going to suggest includes ball bearings, but simple and cheap ones, and the main body of the device is that underrated engineering material, MDF (medium

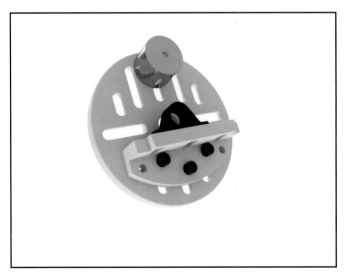

Fig. 10.31 Another typical kit: a faceplate with parallel slots, fitted with its own radiused angle plate. HEMINGWAY KITS

density fibreboard). We won't even be suggesting that you should cut threads, although it might help if you did. How though is the faceplate, or chuck, to be balanced?

All lathes rely on two things to hold a faceplate or a chuck accurately: a register, which comprises a short cylinder of metal concentric with the mandrel it is mounted on and a means of holding and tightening it in place, which in our sizes is a thread and in larger sizes a more complex clamping method. Our balancing spindle will indeed need a register, but the clamping will rely on a separate 'through bolt', nothing more than a length of studding, with washers and nuts – unless, of course, you enjoy the extra challenge and work that cutting a thread to match your lathe will entail. Or perhaps you can find a chuck carrier in the various extras available to match your lathe, with a flange to bolt onto a backplate and a register and thread for the chuck. If you can acquire a suitable fitting, by all means use it and modify my proposal to suit.

The home-made balancing spindle is made from a round mild steel bar slightly larger in diameter than the chuck register and about 30mm long. This is bored to fit on a length (about 250mm) of plain bright mild steel bar (making sure to select a piece that is properly straight), and without changing the settings, machine the outer end of the boss to fit the register in the faceplate. This should produce a bore and a register surface that are truly concentric. As the tool does not need to resist cutting loads, or high speeds, the shaft can be fitted to the boss with

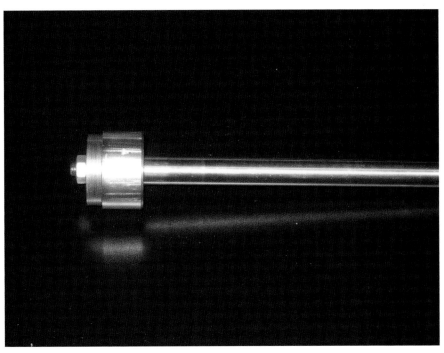

Fig. 10.32 The simple balance shaft, comprising an accurate steel bar carrying a head to match the nose of the lathe mandrel.

bearings, so that it turns with very little resistance. The bearings are held on two plates that are made of MDF about 20mm thick, made up as shown here. The front two bearings carry the main weight of the arbor assembly and the rear two (behind the hole in the MDF) run above the spindle, stopping it from tipping forward. The dimensions are not critical and ordinary bolts or machine screws can be used to hold the bearings, with a washer on each to hold the bearing away from the backplate; just be sure that each bearing of each pair is free to spin on its own, so there needs to be a small gap between them. A really solid location for fairly intensive use might rely on plates of sheet steel or light alloy, perhaps bolted to MDF uprights to keep the cost and weight down, and carrying the bearings. The two plates are held apart so that the bearings line up with your carefully smoothed spindle held horizontally, the front pair of bearings below the spindle and the rear pair above it, with

engineering adhesive; I made mine with a small thread in the end of the spindle and a stud and nut to hold the assembly together.

In use, the faceplate is mounted on the bar by friction alone – and this is where your accurate turning of the register is important. The spindle of the assembly will rest on rolling bearings in use, so before leaving the lathe, spin the spindle and polish its surface with very fine abrasive paper to remove any irregularities.

The resulting assembly or arbor will carry your chuck, or your faceplate, for balancing, but with friction alone holding it together. For added security you can use a stud and washer to hold the faceplate onto the arbor; even better, and much more professional and long lasting, would be to cut a

thread on the boss to match your lathe spindle.

The balancing itself is carried out by resting the mandrel assembly on rolling

Fig. 10.33 Two slabs of MDF, carrying ball bearings on which the balance shaft can spin.

Fig. 10.34 Balancing in operation, with the MDF cradle held firm in a bench vice.

something more presentable, or as an engineering exercise, I hope this basic idea will prompt the necessary thinking processes for your own improvements. You might consider using a mandrel fixed in place permanently in bearings carried in pillow blocks or, for the least possible friction, carry the balancing mandrel on thin discs of hardened steel each carried on a very small ball bearing accurately fitted to its centre.

PRACTICAL APPROACH TO WORK HOLDING A PART WITHOUT DRAWINGS OR INSTRUCTIONS

I know you are not going to need to make what follows. It is added here as an example of the sort of work you might need to carry out, relying simply on a good look at the old part and an understanding of its purpose; it also illustrates the sort of thought processes needed when faced with machining problems for which the best tooling is not obvious. The part is a gear location screw (actually for a 1930 Singer Junior motor car). The tube part holds in place a coil spring and a steel ball, and screws into the lid of the gearbox alongside two others. The balls locate in notches in the selector mechanism to hold the selected gear in place. It is an example of what looks like a fairly simple turning job, but it can be approached in several different ways depending on the tooling available. We will start by looking at which details need to be exactly right, and which are not so fussy. The part serves to hold a ball in place, it is the position of this ball that is critical for the working of the box. The location of the part when fitted in the gearbox

the two plates separated in my case by a softwood block between them, held with woodscrews. The whole contrivance is held steady in the bench vice, or if your vice is too small, the whole thing may be clamped firmly to the bench top.

This holding method is intended to be the simplest of home-made devices relying on a minimum of fancy equipment or parts and a modest level of skill, so inevitably it has a hint of the Heath Robinson about it. You don't know about him? Ask your grandfather, and prepare to be amazed. Should you wish to make

Fig. 10.35 Copying this 1930 car part presents an interesting work-holding problem.

is a problem with this – a lack of the correct gearing with my machine to cut the thread – so the decision is taken to start with a component that is already threaded, a simple machine screw, and work around this.

As a result of this decision, the existing thread itself must be relied upon as the surface for holding the part. Certainly we will not be able to rely on the head of a mass-produced bolt like this being concentric with the thread: just try it if you need to be convinced. Two options come to mind for this holding operation, one relying in this specific case on a ⅝in BSF tap that I just happened to have. The other uses a collet with a bore to match the ⅝in outer diameter of the thread: in practice a 16mm collet works well.

The quicker approach, if you have the right kit to hand, is to use a collet. The reason why a scroll chuck would not be a good idea is that a conventional chuck tends to leave marks – witnesses, we call them – when holding on the top of the thread, but a collet has a much larger area in contact and so can be used with no ill effects. There is a difficulty here though, just as before. While there is no problem holding the work in a 16mm ER collet with the head showing, to turn the head down to the more modest diameter required, how do we hold the workpiece the other way round, with the thread end exposed so we can drill the centre for the spring hole in the tube section? Unless you have a very large collet set, there is no room for the head of the screw inside the holder. Even if we start by milling the end to the required smaller size of hexagon, it still won't fit within the collet holder. All is

Fig. 10.36 Stages in production: the raw screw, head turned down, threads cut away, hole bored, flats machined, with the original part for reference.

is by the threads, so in making a new part the most important detail is to end up with the ball (and therefore the bore in which it sits) central to the threads. The bore must be the right length and

the right size too, and this size needs to be a running clearance on the ball. The best procedure then, might be to turn the threads and to bore the hole at the same settings in the lathe, but there

Fig. 10.37 By a wonderful fluke, the old bearing race was exactly the right diameter.

not lost though, as long as we have a collet holder of the type designed to bolt to a faceplate or a chuck backplate, comprising a thick steel flange with the collet holder as a central extension, so that the big-headed workpiece can be fitted into the collet from the back with no problems. If the head of the part still prevents the collet fixture fitting flat onto the faceplate, it can be spaced away with a short, large-diameter tube with the ends faced off parallel. This

is where good fortune smiled on my endeavours; I found that the register size for the collet holder was exactly right for an old ball bearing race, saving the job of finding a length of tube and machining it.

Once the collet holder assembly has been mounted on the lathe, the inside of the collet holder is centralized using a DTI and a plastic mallet, to ensure that the holder (and the collet and the work) are running truly concentric – after all,

that is how the DTI earns its place in the tool cupboard. Once the vital centre and the spring hole have been drilled in the end of the screw, the process of turning the outside of the tube section can follow, holding the head end in a chuck and the other on the tailstock centre.

The alternative method is to use a tap. This relies on making up a simple tube-jig about 20mm long to hold the screw in the chuck without damaging

Fig. 10.38 Holding a tap between centres provided an extempore jig.

the thread. First though, check that everything else is to hand. The tap itself needs to be sharp. A matching nut will be required, but if this is not available make up a similar but shorter version to use instead of a nut before you make the jig itself and reduce the diameter too – say 10mm thick and 2 or 3mm smaller in diameter. As for material, you will need a length of round bar big enough to take a hole the thread size, perhaps 25mm diameter. Steel, brass or light alloy will

serve. Set the major length of bar firmly in the three-jaw chuck, with perhaps 2 or 3mm extending, and face off the outer surface. Now centre-drill the face, drill through and bore the hole to the tapping size for the thread; this should ensure that the hole is truly concentric with the lathe. In practice, it will be helpful to bore the hole rather bigger than the tapping size, as this will make the next operation, the cutting of the thread itself, quite a lot easier and it will

never need to be fully tightened. Hold the tap in a drill chuck in the tailstock and start the thread by turning the chuck by hand. Once you are sure that the thread is well started, you may find it difficult to grip the tap firmly enough in the drill chuck (especially if you have not made the bore oversize by very much and you are cutting into steel). In this case, it can be helpful to remove the complete chuck, ideally with the tap still in place, to a large bench vice where the whole chuck can be gripped between soft light-alloy jaws. Then you can use a tap holder, relying on the square end of the tap rather than the smooth round surface, and continue the tapping operation right through. Before you do this, check that the hole in the inside end of the chuck is big enough to let the tap enter for a few turns of the thread. When the chuck is returned to the lathe, refit the tap in the thread and turn the chuck by hand as a check. If you find that, despite your best efforts, the thread is not exactly square (in other words, that the centre-line of the tap waves about rather than staying central as it rotates), do not despair. The answer is to use the tap as a mandrel to hold the workpiece between centres in the lathe and drive the tap with a tap-holder on the square end.

Taps are always made with the shank true to the thread and almost always with conventional centres at both ends; this is not for this sort of trick, but for regrinding when they become dulled with much use. The tubular work holder is then skimmed on the outside surface to restore the concentricity. To prevent the work simply screwing along the tap, we use a length of tube over the tap shank to restrain it, choosing a tube that is smaller in outer diameter than the finished size of the workpiece and with its ends properly square to the axis. Then skim the surface of the work holder, taking off as little as possible to produce once more a cylinder concentric and in line with the thread.

Fig. 10.39 Turning the outer surface of a light-alloy mandrel held on the jig.

Before removing the tap, set this newly made jig in the headstock chuck and check that the tap remains central as the chuck is turning. If this is not possible, perhaps because your chuck is past the first flush of youth, you may need to use a four-jaw chuck instead and use a DTI to get things running properly true.

Now we have a simple jig, in which we can start work on the screw, knowing that the thread is true to the lathe axis and so any hole bored in it will also be true. To turn the head down to the across-corners size required, we can use the nut, or alternative work-holder tube, so that the tool is well away from the chuck surface, for instance. The difficulty though, is boring the hole for the spring and turning the threads from the other end to make the tube section. This needs the workpiece fitted from behind the chuck, which is not too difficult now the head has been turned down. But how to prevent the turning operation from unscrewing the work? All we need is the ordinary ⅝in BSF nut, or our home-made alternative, tightened on the working side of the chuck. It can be tightened against the exposed surface of the screw in place in the chuck, using gas pliers for example, as it is only going to be used for this role. This is done first with the minimum of screw thread showing outside the nut. This allows us to make a centre in the end of the thread for support for the next operations. In this case, the centre hole is made rather larger than the spring and ball as this locating surface will be needed for the next operation. Next, drill out to the required depth and ream to the size of the ball. Now remove the holder from the chuck, and

the workpiece from the holder, and fit the workpiece with the newly turned-down head held in the chuck jaws and the newly drilled centre supported by the tailstock. Wonderful, it all runs true! Finish off by turning the outside of the tubular section while the end of the workpiece is supported in this way, as this should ensure that the outside of the tube is concentric with the inner as well as with the thread.

Both these methods leave us with a head with no flats, so cutting them is the final job. A dividing head or rotary table makes this fairly easy, again using a collet to hold the threaded portion or if you are prepared to go gently, only taking small cuts, the tube section can be used to hold the part. In this latter case, add a short piece of silver steel (because it is accurate and strong) inside to reinforce the tube and be sure that the cutting pressure is towards the threaded portion, rather than sideways, as the tube really is quite thin walled. This might mean that the workpiece is held horizontal with the cutter in the vertical mill head and moving towards you with the cutter centralized across the working surface.

First you need to be sure to produce the exact dimension needed across the flats. A micrometer is handiest for this, as when using a calliper the milling head and sharp cutter tend to get in the way. The table (or dividing head) is set to 0 degrees to start and a shaving is taken off, perhaps a maximum of 0.5mm. Then move the table back again in the Y direction and rotate the holder to 180 degrees, leaving the milling head at the same depth setting and take a further shaving off to make

a flat opposite the first one. The cutter is switched off, leaving the height setting as it is, and the table withdrawn towards us, well away from the cutter. Measure the exact AF dimension we now have: subtracting the required AF dimension from this gives the total thickness still to be removed. Half this amount needs to be taken from each of the two faces already cut, so make a note of this amount. Now rotate the work a further 60 degrees (that is, a reading of 240), take a cut without changing the cutter height and do the same at another 60 degrees (that is, at 300), and a further 60 to bring it all back to the zero position. Check that when trying to make another cut, no metal is now removed and you can be sure that nothing has slipped or gone awry. If you were to find that you are cutting metal in this position, you need to stop the work and examine everything carefully to establish exactly what is going wrong. It may not be too late, but you do need to find the error and correct it or you might end up with seven and a half flats – and no spanner in the world will fit that. Two more flats to go, then, at the same initial setting and you are back to 180 degrees. Now the cutter is lowered by another half a millimetre. Go round the six flats in order, taking the same amount off. At this stage it would not hurt to check the AF reading once more, in all three positions, and calculate how much more needs to be removed. Ideally this will now be rather less than half a millimetre, as it was here, so the final cuts are more like a finishing skim. This leaves a burr on the edges next to the threaded section, so a smooth file is used before trying the

Fig. 10.40 Milling the six flats accurately using a collet held by a dividing head. A rotary table would have been just as effective.

part in place in the gearbox. The only difficulty that we skipped over was the possible lack, in your workshop, of a dividing head or rotary table. In the case before us, one answer would be to leave the head turned to the across-corners dimension, then file a wide slot in the top of the head so that it can be tightened with a big screwdriver. After all, although the result will be non-

original, it is just the sort of repair that would have been done when the car was in daily use.

CLAMPING ROUND BAR

When you need to cut a slot or a keyway, in a round bar, there are simple tools that make the job of holding the bar easier. For a flat to locate a cotter, as used to be

fitted in bicycle cranks, the bar can be supported in V-blocks, running in line along the bed of a milling machine or in a fixture as shown here, across the bed, positioning the bar by eye. A keyway, whether a 'feather key' or a 'woodruff key', is a different matter though, as the slot must run exactly in line with the axis of the shaft. In this case, the bar should be held on the machine table

Fig. 10.41 A round bar is held firm in a V-block-cum-angle-plate, so that a slot or keyway can be cut.

resting in a pair of V-blocks, with each block located against a flat bar resting in one of the table slots. Press the bar and its V-blocks firmly into place as you tighten the clamps and check the alignment using a DTI, as described earlier. Hold the woodruff cutter in the mill, extending it in an ER collet holder, if necessary, to clear the clamps or the top of the bar and set it so that the centre of the face of the cutter is at exactly the height of the centre of the bar. This can be calculated from the overall height of the bar from the table, minus half the bar diameter. The cutter should also be located in the X direction exactly in the centre of the desired keyway position. Do not forget to add a firm block bolted down as an end-stop so that the cutter cannot push the bar along instead of cutting and to lock all the adjustments except the Y feed, you are ready to feed the cutter gently into the work. Use plenty of cutting fluid, and if you need to check progress, remember to move the cutter away in the Y direction only, as it will then go back where it came from for the next cuts.

Glossary

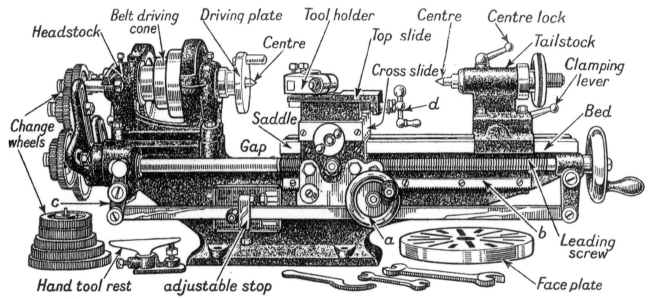

Lathe. Fig. 1. General view of screw cutting 3½ in. lathe capable of turning work up to 3½ in. radius. Work of larger radius may be turned provided it is short enough to rotate in the gap of the bed.

Fig. 11.1 Lathes change as progress continues, but the parts still carry the same names.

Please note that what follows is not intended to offer a full or comprehensive definition of any of the headwords, but it should be enough to give readers a better understanding of technical terms used in the volume and in the trade, and the special engineering senses of some everyday words that may otherwise cause confusion.

123 blocks: hardened steel blocks made accurately with all faces exactly at right angles, with dimensions, traditionally of one, two and three inches, and drilled and tapped with an array of holes so that they can be used to make up small angle plates and similar fixtures, as well as in identical pairs or singly. Similar versions are available in metric sizes, but they still carry a name blessed with faint echoes of empire.

AF, Across Flats: the conventional way to designate a hexagonal or square bar, or the size of a bolt or screw head, and the spanner to fit it. The term is also used in a restricted sense to refer to threaded parts made to US or Unified standards, where the spanner sizes are designated with an AF dimension in inches and sixteenths. Confusion can arise with spanners in Whitworth and BSF sizes, which are also designated in fractions of an inch, but referring to the diameter of the standard bolt rather than the bolt-head.

Angle blocks: a set of hard steel blocks or slabs, normally about 5mm thick, made with sides machined and ground exactly to a range of (small) angles so that work can be positioned and

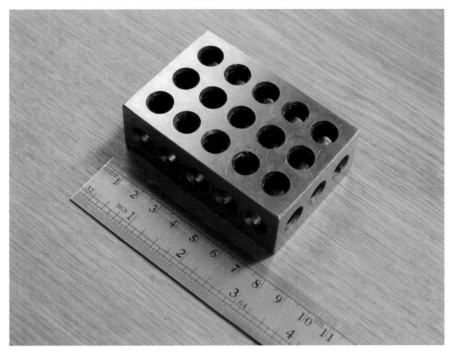

Fig. 11.2 A steel 123 block is ground to accurate dimensions. Some of the holes are tapped, others plain, so that angle blocks can be made up.

clamped in a known orientation. The full set usually ranges from one degree to ten, with the smaller angles in half-degree stages.

Angle plate: an L-shaped or corner-shaped fitting, usually of cast iron, machined accurately at a right angle and with all the outer edges machined square. The faces have through slots, or T-slots, so that work can be clamped accurately at right angles to the table of a machine. Even more useful are the versions machined accurately on the inside faces too, but they are not so easy to find.

Apron: the part of a lathe carriage that connects the toolpost and the saddle to the lead screw. It faces the operator and usually carries the manual horizontal feed, a lever to engage the lead screw and a thread indicator.

Arbors: also called Mandrels, these tools are used to hold rotary saws and similar small tools, and for machining parts with circular holes. They are made from steel, often accurately hardened and ground, with a taper to fit a lathe or mill and often with a thread and nut, and a keyway in the cylindrical section to locate parts securely. The rotating spindle of a lathe or milling machine is also sometimes called the arbor.

Fig. 11.3 By combining two or more of these steel plates, a wide range of angles can be made up for setting tools, vices and similar roles. ARC EURO TRADE LTD

Axis (pl. axes): each of the three primary directions in which a tool can move in relation to a workpiece. Informally, they are left and right, to and fro, and up and down. More formally, they are referred to by the letters X, Y and Z, with a positive movement respectively, being to the right, away from you, and upwards. Once a datum point has been established, any position away from this can be identified by stating its 'coordinates', which means the three dimensions X, Y and Z each measured from the zero point. When writing this down, the negative or minus sign should not be overlooked, it is better to add a plus (+) whenever appropriate to reduce confusion. The term 'axis' is also used for the line around which a spindle or similar part rotates.

Barrel chuck: a thick-walled tube of steel with radial bolts and an accurately cylindrical outer surface. This can be clamped using the bolts onto an irregular part so that it can be carried in a steady when turning. Very early lathes had a similar arrangement with a taper, or threaded fitting at one end, for use as a chuck.

Bed: the generally flat-machined surface of a lathe extending from the headstock and extending past the tailstock. The carriage and toolpost assembly runs along the bed and is located by the 'shears', extensions formed in the casting and machined to give accurate locating surfaces.

Black (steel): some commercial steel is usually offered in two finishes: black and bright. Black steel has a rough,

Fig. 11.4 *Black steel (top) is not just a different surface finish, it is less accurate to size and harder to machine.*

blackish surface, which is likely to show grooves and other markings from manufacture. Bright steel comes with a much smoother, flatter, metallic finish, with sharper edges and very few visible flaws. Bright steel is preferred for machining, but black material can be used although it takes longer to get an acceptable flat, or smooth, surface. Nuts and bolts in larger sizes are also supplied in black or bright finish.

Bright (steel): *see* Black.

Burr: a sharp edge of material that forms mainly on the trailing edge of a machined or filed component. Any burr should be removed by careful filing or stoning before carrying out further work on the part. The term burr is also used for small tools made of tool steel or

carbide, resembling tiny milling cutters but more like files in operation. They are used in die-grinders and small high-speed, hand-held electric machines, of which the best-known is the Dremel.

Carbide: a cutting tool material made from complex mixtures of carbides of tungsten and other metals, which are harder and more heat resistant than high-speed steel, but which lack their toughness. Small slabs of carbide are used as cutting edges, fixed to steel tools by brazing or as carefully shaped inserts attached by threaded fasteners. Milling cutters and drills can also be made from solid carbide. In chemical terms a carbide is a compound of a metal (or a similar substance, such as silicon) with carbon.

Fig. 11.5 A typical selection of centres to fit MT2 tapers.

applied, often without distinction, to the pointed end, the conical hole and to the tool itself.

Centre drill: a short round bar of tool steel ground at both ends for drilling holes to locate on centres. The tip is a small diameter, short drill, which widens into a 60-degree countersink. A range of sizes is available from 3mm to 12mm or more. As well as drilling holes to locate centres, they are useful in the smaller sizes for 'spotting' a hole when using a mill as a jig-borer for marking out. Special longer versions are available for cases where access is difficult.

Centre pop: a small conical depression made with a centre punch as a guide for drilling or when marking dimensions on a workpiece.

Centre punch: a steel tool with a sharp conical point used for marking metal in preparation for further work. The points are usually ground at 90 degrees for starting a drill, but at 60 degrees for marking out.

Change wheels: a set of gear wheels provided as part of the equipment of a lathe, to allow a wide range of thread pitches to be cut by changing the gear ratio of the lead screw. They are often also used as counterweights when turning eccentric parts on the faceplate, as each size is, conveniently, a different weight.

Chuck: a rotating holder for tools or components, made of steel, with slots containing steel sliding jaws that can

Carriage: The assembly forming the part of a lathe that slides between the headstock and tailstock. It comprises the saddle and apron (sometimes made in one piece), and carries the cross-slide on its upper surface, this in turn carries the top slide and toolpost.

Centre: the conical mounting points that can be fitted to the head- and tailstock of a lathe to hold a workpiece or as a guide to machining operations. Centres are normally made of hardened steel and sometimes with carbide tips for wear resistance in extended work, but soft steel versions are useful in some cases. For work close to the end of the workpiece, a 'half-centre' can be useful: a flat is ground off at one side almost to the middle of the centre. The term is be moved together or apart to provide grip. Most chucks are opened and closed with a key comprising a male square on a bar with a T-handle. Small chucks often have a knurled ring with tommy-bar holes rather than the more elaborate square hole and key.

Clamping bar: a rectangular steel bar with a central slot; one end is sometimes milled with zigzag grooves. They are used with T-nuts, studs and raising blocks to hold work firmly in place on a milling table or on a faceplate.

Coach bolt: a threaded fastener with a shallow domed head, beneath which is a squared section.

Cross-slide: the part of a lathe toolpost assembly that can move across the saddle at right angles to the working axis. The toolpost is fixed above it, sometimes on a separate slide that can be set to an angle other than 90 degrees.

Dial gauge: a measuring tool with a central plunger, movement of which is shown by a pointer on a dial. The gearing and spindles are accurately made so that very small movements can be shown and measured consistently. A DTI is similar, but relies on movement of a lever rather than a plunger.

Dividing: the process in which a part can be rotated successively by exact amounts and held so that machining operations can be carried out. A dividing head will allow the full-turn rotation to be divided into a very wide range of divisions – from the four or six sides of a bolt-head to the many

Fig. 11.6 The larger versions of dial gauge, shown here give exact readings of the plunger movement, while the smaller version is a DTI, operated by a short lever and is sensitive, rather than exact.

divisions around a lathe toolpost feed dial, or the multiple teeth of gears used in clocks and similar devices. A dividing head also has the capability of being tilted and locked in position so that the chuck, or similar, can be vertical, horizontal or any angle between.

Dog: A special clamp fixed at one end of a part being turned between centres

so that it can be driven round by a peg or a slot on the faceplate. Also called a carrier.

Drawbar or Draw-bolt: a round bar of steel with a square and a cylindrical boss at one end and a thread at the other, fitted inside the arbor of a milling machine or a lathe, and used to tighten a tool in place in the taper. The boss is

Fig. 11.7 The workings of this device are exactly the same as a digital caliper; it allows movement of the bed to be measured directly, in inches or millimetres.

trapped within a tube nut at the outer end of the spindle so that taper fittings can be loosened by unscrewing the bar.

DRO, Digital Read-Out: an electronic measuring device connected to one of the three axes of a mill or similar machine. Movement of the tool in relation to the table is shown in decimal form, usually to 0.005mm or 0.001inches. Greater precision is also available at rather higher cost.

DTI, Dial Test Indicator: an inspection tool comprising a small lever or arm that rests on the work, and a dial with a pointer that moves to show the smallest movements of the lever tip. Normally held in a clamp on a magnetic stand, it is very useful to ensure, for example, that rotating parts are truly concentric and to indicate by how much they need adjusting to centre them properly.

Eccentric: any part that rotates around an axis that is not its centre-line is eccentric. The term is used as a noun to describe the out-of-centre discs used on the crankshafts of steam engines to operate the valve gear. The action is the same as a crank with a very large crankpin.

Elastic Limit: whenever a force is applied to a solid, distortion takes place. This distortion can be temporary,

Fig. 11.8 Whenever you need to check the width of a narrow gap, feeler gauges are indispensable.

with the shape returning to the original as the force is removed. If the stress exceeds a certain amount, the distortion can be permanent or the material may break apart. This certain amount of stress is called the elastic limit of the material. Strong metals like steel have a high elastic limit, which means they are difficult to distort or break.

Feeler gauge: flat strips of shim stock marked with their thickness, used to check very thin spaces and adjustments. Sets of blades arranged like a penknife are available in inch and in metric dimensions.

Flat: flats are the plane surfaces made (usually by filing or machining) on a part to which a dog is fixed for turning between centres and similar work, or to fix a pulley to a shaft with a grub screw and (by machining) on both sides of a cylindrical part so it can be held with a spanner. The flats on commercial nuts and bolts are generally made by pressing in a tool-steel die.

Fly-cutter: a rotating tool with a single cutter set to describe a fairly large radius, used when milling to produce a flat surface over a large area.

Friction: the resistance to sliding movement caused when two surfaces are pressed together. When sliding occurs, heat is produced and this is why cutting tools and workpieces get hot. Friction can also cause wear.

Gap-bed: in some lathes, the bed is cut away at the headstock end to allow for larger, but short, workpieces to be turned and to permit the fitting of a larger than usual faceplate.

Gauge blocks or Slip gauges: sets comprising a range of hardened steel blocks ground very accurately to a series of thicknesses. By combining blocks from a full set and 'wringing' them together, any length can be created, in accurate steps of 0.005mm or 0.0001inches. One use for these expensive sets is in setting up a sine bar to a precise angle.

Gauge plate: good quality tool steel plate that is ground accurately flat on both faces; also known as ground flat stock, it is widely available in thickness from 1 to 10mm and similar inch sizes. It can be used in the annealed (soft) state as it is supplied for making tools that require accuracy and resistance to damage, it can be hardened and tempered using the same techniques as for silver steel.

Gib strip: the sliding parts of lathes and milling machines are usually carried on interlocking dovetails of metal. Allowance for assembly and wear is provided by adding a gib strip, a long thin strip of metal to form the rubbing surface on one side of the slot with, in some versions, an adjustment formed by a row of grub screws, or in others by using a slightly tapered slot with a slightly tapered gib strip located endways by screws.

Half-centre: *see* Centre.

Fig. 11.9 Gauge blocks or slip gauges are used in the same way as feeler gauges, but for gaps wider than 1mm. They also find use when setting a sine bar accurately to a given angle.

High-speed steel: alloys of steel that include small percentages of metals, such as nickel, tungsten, molybdenum, vanadium, manganese and chromium. These retain a very hard and tough cutting edge at high temperatures, enabling continuous high speeds to be used in machining processes.

Horizontal mills: generally much larger than hobby sizes, a horizontal mill has a rotating mandrel carried in the Y direction. Cutters like very chunky circular saw blades are carried on the mandrel. To change the depth of cut, the table can move up and down, as well as in the more normal X and Y directions.

Index: a scale with markings denoting a distance or angle, as found on a rotary table or an adjusting screw. An indexing plunger is used to lock a device, such as a dividing head, in a fixed position; and an indexing head is a small, relatively simple dividing head with a limited number of positions and a fixture to take collets for holding a workpiece.

Indexable: as applied to tooling relates to the use of cutters with carbide inserts, accurately made so that a worn or damaged insert can be replaced without reducing the precision of the work.

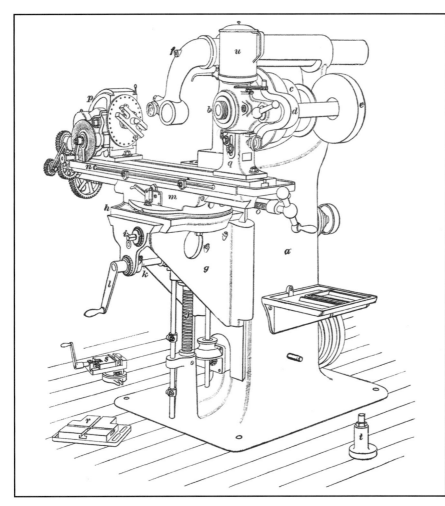

Fig. 11.10 This horizontal mill uses cutters carried on a removable mandrel fitting into the socket (b).

Knee: on some larger milling machines the head that carries the tool is fixed in the Z direction (so no up and down movement) and instead the table is moved up and down, carrying with it the workpiece. The device that controls this movement is called the knee.

Leverage: the process whereby a small force acting on a bar can produce a large force by careful positioning of the pivot. In many contexts this term can mean the same as torque and in physics is the same as moment, a combination of force and distance.

Live: a live centre is one that can rotate on its own internal bearings, as distinct from a dead centre (which can't). The term can also be used for a centre that is driven, as in the headstock of a lathe, as distinct from one fixed in a tailstock.

Lubrication: the use of fluids (or finely divided solids) to reduce the friction between surfaces in contact and to reduce the heat and wear resulting from sliding.

Jig: a device made to hold work for machining operations, so that it can be held more firmly, or more accurately, or to attach to it in order to locate holes accurately or to simplify and speed up repetitive operations.

Jig-borer: a large vertical mill designed for the accurate drilling and boring operations needed to make jigs and for similar work. The position of the table in relation to the cutting tool is accurately controlled with dials and scales so that precise work positioning can be carried out. A smaller mill fitted with DROs can serve a similar role in the home workshop.

Key steel: square bars of mild steel intended as stock for making rectangular keys. Made to accurate sizes in inch and metric dimension, and sold in the work-hardened condition, key steel can form the basis for home-made raising blocks and spacers when locating parts on a worktable.

Mandrel: the hollow spindle of a lathe or milling machine, which is driven by the motor and carries the chuck, tool holder and so on. The term is also applied to any commercial or custom-made circular device for holding a part or tool, and is another name for an arbor.

Micrometer: a precise tool used for measuring the distances between two outer surfaces and the thicknesses of parts. Normally looking rather like a

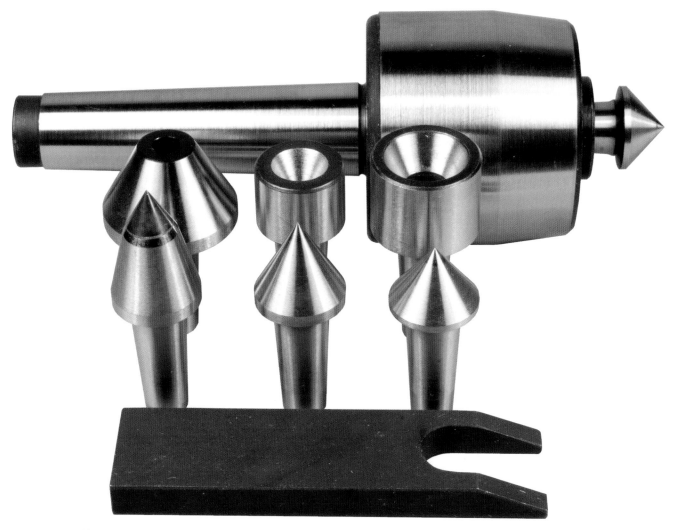

Fig. 11.11 This set of fittings for a live centre includes a carbide tip and a range of tip angles, including internal cones that are very handy for holding tubes.
ARC EURO TRADE LTD

precision-made G-clamp, they are made in a range of sizes to measure from 0 to 25mm upwards. Sizes over about 100mm can be very expensive and so are not common. Similar tools with the same fine-thread measuring spindles are also made, for example as depth and bore gauges, and for specialized jobs like measuring gear teeth.

Morse Taper, MT: the most common standard series of tapers used to hold tools in place in the headstocks and tailstocks of smaller lathes, and in milling machines. They range from MT0 to MT7; common sizes found in smaller hobby-sized machines are MT2 (17.8mm at the large end) and MT3 (23.8mm).

Normal: at right angles, usually in relation to a plane surface.

Normalized: when steel is normalized in heat treatment, usually by holding for a set time at an elevated temperature, this removes internal stresses and produces a desirable fine-grained crystal structure, ready for further operations including hardening without distortion.

Fig. 11.12 An English metric 0 to 25mm micrometer, a Japanese 1 to 2 inch model and, between them, a version with a separate anvil that can be changed for a rod to measure the wall thickness of tube.

cold water, or oil, or using an air blast. Steel can be toughened while retaining hardness if this is done carefully; other metals, such as copper or brass, are softened by quenching.

Quill: on a vertical mill, the quill is the rotating arbor that carries the cutting tool. It can be moved up and down within a tube that turns in bearings. The tube is driven by the motor with the drive transmitted to the quill by splines.

Race: the steel rings forming the inner and outer parts of a ball or roller bearing assembly. They have surfaces that are hard and usefully precise, and can be put to use in a machine shop, for example as accurate spacers, even when the bearings themselves are worn out.

Raising blocks: hardened steel rectangular blocks accurately made in matching pairs to position work above a table or similar surface. This is a common use for 123 blocks. Where precision is not so vital, similar blocks made from offcuts can be useful.

Origin: when marking out work, or using a mill as a jig borer, the origin is the point at which the X, Y and Z dimensions are all zero – in other words the starting point for measurements, usually at the left side of the part so that most dimensions are positive. Some older drawings are not dimensioned in this way and this can lead to cumulative errors.

Parallel: used as a noun to describe a block of hardened steel with precisely ground and parallel faces, often used in pairs to support work, and when marking out and so on.

Quenching: sudden cooling of hot steel (or other metal) from red heat, for instance by plunging the part into

Fig. 11.13 A modestly priced set of pairs of parallels, accurately ground to size on the top and bottom surfaces. ARC EURO TRADE LTD

Register: a locating shoulder, for example one turned on a backplate on the lathe it will be used with, to locate a bolted chuck or similar tool so that it is accurately in line and concentric.

Resultant: when two or more forces act on anything, they combine to produce a stress or a movement (or both) in the direction of the resultant force. The strength and direction of the resultant force can be calculated from the relative strengths and directions of the original forces.

Rotary table: a fitting carrying a circular plate with slots for a chuck or clamping devices, which can be bolted down on a milling table with its face set horizontally or vertically. The plate can usually be rotated by winding a handle at the side, the amount of rotation is shown in degrees so that accurate angles can be set. A rotary table is in effect a simpler version of a dividing head but without the tilting function.

Saddle: the central movable part of a lathe. It sits over the bed and is guided by it; it carries the cross-slide and the toolpost slide at the top, the apron hangs down towards the operator.

Scroll: a circular plate of metal inside a chuck mechanism, which is rotated by the chuck key and moves the jaws. The working surface of the plate has a spiral groove (like a very coarse gramophone disc) in which teeth on the jaws engage, moving the jaws in and out.

Shears: the locating surfaces on a lathe bed that control the position of the saddle and the tailstock. They may be the flat edges of the bed or angled ridges on the bed surface. The accuracy of the machine relies on them being precisely machined, unworn and undamaged.

Shims: strips or sheets of very thin metal, usually steel or brass, made in precise thicknesses throughout. Their uses include making minor adjustments of position between clamped surfaces. The thicknesses of shim stock readily available range from 0.05mm (0.002in) upwards.

Silver steel: a carbon steel that is readily available in accurately ground bars and is useful for making spindles and tools. It can be hardened and tempered without sophisticated temperature control and is named from its colour; it does not contain silver.

Sine bar: a steel bar with accurately ground angled locations at both ends. In each of these corners a ground steel cylinder is fixed, both of the same size exactly. In use one cylinder of the bar rests on a flat surface (the table of a mill, for example) and the cylinder at the other end is supported on a column of accurately sized spacers called gauge blocks. A calculation is made to set the angle precisely using the sine of the angle, knowing the distance the cylinders are apart and the height of the gauge block column.

Fig. 11.14 For use with machines at the smallest end of the hobby range, this baby tool lacks the worm drive of its bigger brothers. AXMINSTER TOOL CENTRE LTD

Slip gauges: another name for gauge blocks.

Fig. 11.15 This is the working side of the scroll. The reverse has a bevel crown-wheel turned by smaller pinions operated by the chuck key.

Slitting: the machining of accurate thin slots, such as those in a taper collet, with a mill or a lathe, using a rotating slitting saw carried on an arbor.

Smooth: files are made with teeth in a wide range of sizes, ranging from the coarsest, called Bastard, through Second cut, to Smooth (and even finer cuts). The term is confusing because a smooth file will still cut metal although it produces fine filings and a fairly smooth surface.

Spot- or Spotting-drill: a short drill-bit, often with a 90-degree point, used to mark a workpiece through the holes in another already drilled part clamped to it, in preparation for further drilling or similar operations. Spotting drills are also available with carbide tips for use on very hard materials.

Fig. 11.16 Set up here on a granite surface plate, a sine bar can be set to any angle from 0 to almost 90 degrees, by changing the height of the column of slips.

Fig. 11.17 These slitting saws all have the same 1in bore, an important detail if you want to avoid buying several sizes of mandrel.

Steady: a fixture that can be carried by the saddle of a lathe (a travelling steady) or clamped to the bed (a fixed steady), with supports for holding work central that cannot be supported in the tailstock, and to support the central section of a long or flexible part during turning between centres.

Surface plate: a flat block of cast iron, or granite, accurately machined over (at least) the top surface and used for marking out and checking dimensions, using the flat surface as a datum face.

Swarf: the shreds and ribbons of ragged metal produced in turning and milling processes. The edges and points of swarf are very sharp and will readily embed themselves in skin and clothing unless great care is taken (and sometimes even then).

T-nuts, T-slots: the cross-slide of a lathe and the table of a mill and column drill are usually provided with clamping slots with the section of an inverted T. Special nuts that fit the slots closely are added, so that studs can be used to clamp work in place, or to hold a vice, a rotary table, an angle plate and so on. A wide range of slot sizes and threads have been used over the years and it is important to use the size of T-nut that fits your slots properly, as anything smaller may overload and damage the edges of the slot.

Table: the flat horizontal surface of a mill or similar machine on which the work is carried either directly using clamps or using a vice or similar fixture and held in place by studs and T-nuts in longitudinal slots. The table on a small mill can be moved in the X and Y directions, while on larger industrial mills movement of the table in the Z direction is also possible.

Tailstock: the part of a lathe, usually at the right of the bed, which can be moved along the bed and (usually) adjusted sideways for alignment. The central spindle is (usually) bored to a Morse Taper so that a centre or a tool such as a drill can be held firmly and centrally to the chuck, a handle on the outer end allows the spindle to be moved towards the headstock for drilling, boring and similar operations. A Rolling Tailstock arbor carries a centre with a ball-bearing attachment carrying a chuck that can rotate freely. This can be used to support a tube, for example during turning, when a normal centre cannot be used.

Fig. 11.18 If you use a rotary table with its axis horizontal, a tailstock is vital to support the work. This version is adjustable in height. AXMINSTER TOOL CENTRE LTD

Temper, tempering: steel that can be hardened has to go through two processes to be useful. Hardening involves heating red-hot and quenching; the exact temperature, timing and quenching method depends mainly on the grade of steel. This can produce extreme hardness, but the result is not at all tough, so the hardness is modified (tempered) by heating again to a much lower temperature. This reduces the hardness only slightly, but increases the toughness a lot. The term is also applied to the degrees of hardness produced in some aluminium alloys by work- or solution-hardening operations.

Tommy-bar: a tough rod of steel used for tightening for example, in place of a spanner or key when a round hole is provided in the tooling.

Tool steel: alloys of steel that can be hardened to a high degree while retaining toughness, both of which

Fig. 11.19 Whenever you need a parallel firm grip, these toolmaker's clamps can be used.

Tramming: the process by which the head of a milling machine for example, is adjusted so that the spindle is exactly at right angles to the table. If the head is designed, as many are, so that the head can be offset to an angle and clamped in place, or with a column that can be angled at the base. It can be susceptible to a hard knock, so it is important to check the tramming whenever accurate work is required and especially after heavy work, an interrupted cut or a tool-jam, any of which can cause the head to lose its position. For some mills it is not just a matter of a minor adjustment of screws to put things right, but the addition of shims between clamped faces.

V-block: A tool steel block, usually a cube, with accurate ground V-shaped notches in its faces, used as a support for round parts when machining. They are usually supplied in matching pairs, with clamps to fit around the work.

Toolmaker's vice: a solidly made machine vice with all faces ground accurately flat and parallel, making it useful in a range of holding positions.

Vernier: a measuring scale calibrated in inches or millimetres like a steel rule, but with a further scale sliding along it.

are retained at high temperatures. Steels that include iron and carbon only, such as 'silver steel', require only simple hardening and tempering, but lose their hardness at relatively low temperatures (from 300°C) so most production steel cutting tools are now made from high-speed steel, which includes additional alloying elements, such as chromium, nickel, tungsten and molybdenum.

Toolmaker's clamp: a pair of square steel bars is fitted with fine thread screws so that they can be tightened together over a wide range of sizes while remaining reasonably parallel. One screw is used to adjust the size, the other to tighten the clamp. They are often kept in pairs and adjusted in use to be as nearly parallel as possible, as this spreads the clamping load over a wide area of the workpiece.

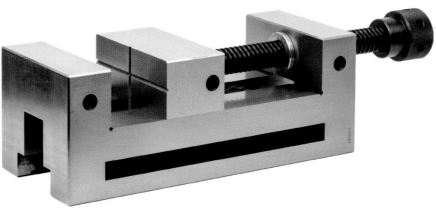

Fig. 11.20 Several styles of toolmaker's vice are available, with differing clamp systems. ARC EURO TRADE LTD

Fig. 11.21 Sizes of V-block range from about 40mm cube to 150mm or more, often with the larger sizes in cast iron. ARC EURO TRADE LTD

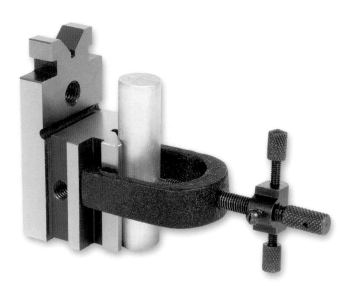

Fig. 11.22 A more adaptable V-block style, sometimes called a universal or toolmaker's V-block. AXMINSTER TOOL CENTRE LTD

Vice: a work-holding tool with parallel flat faces that can be moved together to hold work for machining. Whereas a woodworker's vice is fixed to the bench, a machining vice is a separate component that is bolted or clamped in place to suit the work in progress. A drill vice is relatively lightweight and is often held on the drill platform by hand, while a milling vice needs to be much stronger and heavier, and it must be clamped down. A toolmaker's vice, also used to hold work for milling, is ground accurately flat and parallel on all sides and can be used in a range of orientations. Vices with angle and swivelling fixtures are also available for more specialized milling.

Wringing: the process in which gauge blocks are cleaned and then pressed together by hand with a rotating motion, so that air is excluded and the two adjacent faces are truly in contact. This requires a mirror-like finish on both parts in contact. That is one reason why gauge blocks are expensive and why they should always be used and stored very carefully. When properly wrung together, gauge blocks will remain together until they are wrung apart. This ensures convenience and stability, as well as a high level of precision in use.

X, Y and Z: *see* Axis

Extra precision is achieved by noting the exact alignment of the two scales. Sliding callipers offering internal, external and depth measurements are traditionally fitted with vernier scales, and this has led to them being called 'verniers', even extending the term to modern callipers of similar design fitted with electronic readouts rather than the traditional vernier scale.

Useful Addresses

In compiling this volume, the following firms have been particularly helpful, and my thanks are extended to them all:

Arc Euro Trade Ltd
10 Archdale Street, Syston, Leicester
LE7 1NA
www.arceurotrade.co.uk

Axminster Tool Centre Ltd
Unit 10 Weycroft Avenue, Axminster,
Devon EX13 5PH
www.axminster.co.uk

Hemingway Kits
126 Dunval Road, Bridgnorth,
Shropshire WV16 4LZ
www.hemingwaykits.com

In the modern age of electronic communications, the ready availability of information has improved immensely, while at the same time suppliers and their details tend to change frequently. It would be nugatory trying to offer a list of suppliers that may well be up to date as we go to press, but which may be out of date before you read it. A search of the Web under the key 'Model Engineering Supplies' will bring up a wide range of useful addresses. Further information may be found by searching for 'Model Engineering Magazines' and 'Model Engineering Clubs'; many of those found under these headings have their own websites too.

Index

Other Crowood Metalworking Titles

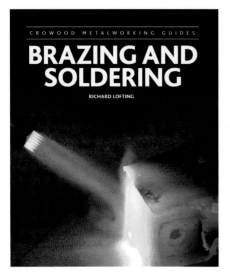

Brazing and Soldering 978 1 84797 836 3

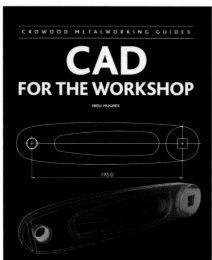

CAD for the Workshop 978 1 84797 566 9

CNC Milling in the Workshop 978 1 84797 512 6

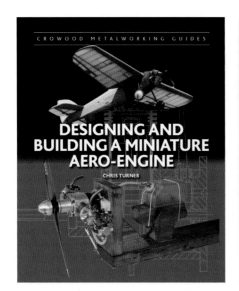

Designing and Building a Model Aero-Engine
978 1 84797 776 2

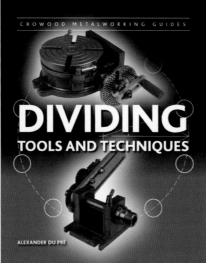

Dividing 978 1 84797 776 838 7

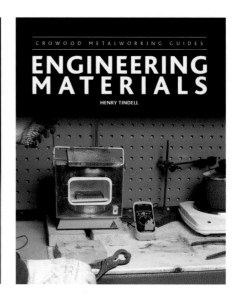

Engineering Materials 978 1 84797 679 6

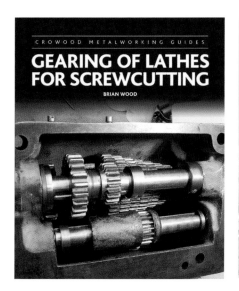

Gearing of Lathes for Screwcutting
978 1 78500 250 2

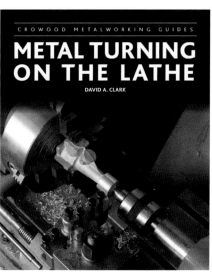

Metal Turning on the Lathe 978 1 84797 523 2

Milling 978 1 84797 774 8

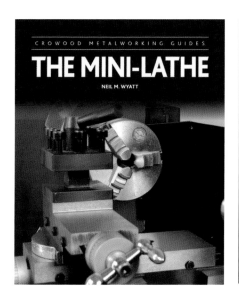

The Mini-Lathe 978 1 78500 128 4

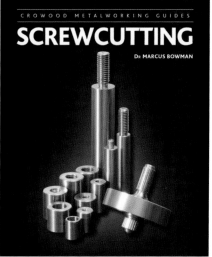

Screwcutting 978 1 84797 999 5

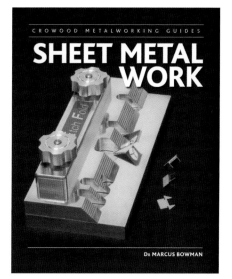

Sheet Metal Work 978 1 84797 778 6